MW00604712

Asian American Anthology:
I Am An American Too

by Hyun Martin, Mark Hagland, Aryani Ong,

Henry Lee, Phil Tajitsu Nash, Tonia Bui,

Hoan Dang, Ai-Ling Louie,

Lily Liu, Susan C. Lee, et al

Copyright

Copyright © 2021 Hyun Martin, all rights reserved.

The stories are submitted by Asian Americans of their lived experiences in America. Each contributor retains their copyright to their own work. No part of this book may be reproduced, or stored in a retrieval system, or transmitted in any form or by any means, electronic, mechanical, photocopying, recording, or otherwise, without express written permission of the publisher or the individual contributor.

Rufina C. Garay photo by Michael Thee

hyun@hyunmartin.com

ISBN: 978-1-947235-02-1

Cover design by: Julie Seaward

Library of Congress Control Number: 2018675309

Printed in the United States of America. 61,600 words.

10 Original Founders

Thank You to the original group of nine friends: Mark Hagland; Ai-Ling Louie; Lily Liu; Phil Tajitsu Nash, JD; Senator Susan C. Lee, JD; Henry Lee, DDS; Aryani Ong, JD; Tonia Bui and Hoan Dang.

Preface

On a day last Spring, 2020, 34-year-old Bawi Cung was grocery shopping at a Sam's Club in Midland, Texas with his sons, who were five and two. He was confronted by a man who grabbed a knife from a nearby rack. Cung was slashed on his face, his 2-year-old was stabbed in the back, and his 5-year-old was stabbed in the face.

The attacker, 19 year old Jose' Gomez, was stopped by an off-duty Border Patrol Agent, Bernie Ramirez, who identified himself as law enforcement and drew his weapon. Ramirez, and at least three other people who tried to intervene, were also injured.

Why did the attacker choose Cung and his children? He later said he thought they were Chinese, and he blamed them for the coronavirus, alternately referred to at that time by then-President Donald Trump as the "China Virus" and the "Kung Flu." Cung, incidentally, is NOT Chinese, he is from Myanmar. But that wasn't the point; the point was that he was Asian, and the attack against him demonstrated the damage that hate, racial-profiling, and discrimination against Asians, heightened during the Covid-19 pandemic, has poisoned our society.

A year later, despite suffering the external injuries and the emotional traumas of the attack, (his sons still bear these scars as well), Cung said he still wanted to be a American in "an America that respects people."

When I learned about the Cung case, I was inspired, incensed, disheartened, and traumatized all at once. I grew up in Texas. As a Korean-adoptee who came to the US in the '60's, the Cung story hit me hard. This was not the Texas I grew up in. Candidly, this was not the America I grew up in; today's America is so different!

Hate crimes against Asian Americans have been multiplying; they are a stain that must be addressed. I wanted to do something about it. I turned to ten of my fellow Asian-Americans, friends with whom I have discussed this issue. We decided to develop the "Asian-American Anthology: I Am An American Too."

One of the goals was to focus on non-violent communication. One of the questions that needed to be answered in order to create an understanding among races was "What happened to you?" Other questions included "Why are you sitting in judgment and hatred?" "How can we support each other facing the trauma of Hate Crimes?" "How can we feel safe?" If people can shelve their hatred long-enough to be open to communication, maybe we can finally come to an understanding and live in that America that Cung referred to as "an America that respects people."

Non-Violent Communication

We are telling our stories so you can relate to us, so you can learn to connect with other people who don't necessarily look like you. We want you to learn how to build an understanding with people so no one turns to violence and hatred to confront their issues.

A year after the attack on himself and his two young boys, Bawi Cung said he had forgiven his attacker. He wanted to move on and heal, both physically and emotionally. He forgave his attacker, and he was able to "pay-it-forward," to teach other people to build bridges even in the face of what seemed to be insurmountable pain. Essentially, he said "we are all human," let's get past our differences, let's understand them, and let's find a way to live together.

Non-violent communication can be achieved when we allow ourselves to say what we're feeling, when we own what we're feeling and when we take responsibility for our actions. It requires us, first and foremost, to listen to the other person, to acknowledge what they're saying and to mirror it back to them. In other words, "I understand what you are saying; did I get it? Or is there something else you wanted me to hear?"

Someone expressing themselves through this nonviolent communication says:

"When you do X (action, tone, expression); I feel Y (emotion); I need Z (needs: safety, validation, respect, support, love, etc.) and I request that you do Action (new behavior) instead to communicate. We all have free will choice. If they refuse to honor your request then you know they can't honor the relationship or they may fail. It's also a way to see if there is progress. People fail but do they clean it up by acknowledging it with, " I'm sorry. Please forgive me. Thank you. I love you." Hoponnonno prayer. I like to use the violet flame to transmute and transform any situation after doing my best in any situation to communicate honestly my feelings, my needs and my requests.

I have been on a 7 1/2 months of forgiveness and communicating to repair a relationship with my college sweetheart. We have both done the work of acknowledging and apologizing for our part in the breakdown of our 9-year relationship. We were 17 and 18 and so immature and insecure to be in a loving relationship. We tried, but didn't know how to understand ourselves and each other. Now we have a much better understanding and realize the maturity and growth in skills to have an honest loving relationship that we didn't have 40 + years ago.

This is my hope for all people to begin to clean up and work on repairing through a Truth and Reconciliation meetings that South Africa had after Apartheid. I believe we in America need to also have this to heal our nation.

Earth Angels

Martin Luther King Jr. said, "Don't let them get you to hate them!" That's why I believe in seeing the humanity in everyone. Which is why curiosity and wanting to listen with compassion instead of judgment works. I believe in the power of questions to allow everyone to be hooked into conversations of understanding and building common ground. I must confess that I retreated into my bubble during the reign of 45.

However while Democracy is always on the line, I do believe enough of us have woken to the fact that Democracy must be exercised by the People to make it for the People again instead of special interests. It truly needs to be about all Americans can be lifted by sharing and caring both locally, state, nationally and internationally.

I am on a mission to create what I like to call "Earth Angels." When you open your heart, when you listen, when you are able to fully express your feelings and truly understand what another person is feeling you can become an "Earth Angel." You may not agree with what the other person is saying, but you can create a connection with this person simply by allowing them to express themselves, truly listening, and letting that person know you are hearing them and seeking to understand them. When you create this connection with another person, you both become more grounded with each other and with the earth. This is why I call those who practice this form of non-violent communication "Earth Angels."

I believe that the majority of people have been acting out from fear which is the absence of love. If we are to heal our nation and our earth, we get to open our hearts and keep choosing love over fear and hate. I truly believe if we all choose love, we will want to be supported, to feel loved, to be safe and secure, to be respected, validated and honored for our value and for our humanity. We all want a future that is more equitable, a society where everyone feels they have a shot at the American dream; that we all matter. We all want a peaceful country of "Earth Angels" who support each other. We should all want and choose to be part of this mission of each pursuing our vision of love and as long as it doesn't hurt people or other creatures, I'm OK with you pursuing your dreams. I just want a world that understands a sustainable life and living for both the good of ancestors and descendants. I am enclosing forgiveness prayers, so we can do a reset and start over in building trust and communication again. Hugs and blessings!

— *Hyun Martin*

Hyun Martin

Coming Full Circle to 1967 in 2020

When I was a child of 5, I wanted so much to have blonde long curly hair and blue eyes like Elly May of Beverly Hillbillies! That was just what I felt like coming from the Ozarks Hills and for me, Inchon, South Korea: outhouse, one room cabin and you ate whatever you grew caught or shot. I came from a third world country, Inchon and Seoul, South Korea. My birth family did live in a small Korean style home. Mr. Drysdale tried to get the Clampetts to join high society, but they didn't change themselves or their country ways. Elly May and sometimes Jethro would get more citified and civilized, but they would go back to what was comfortable for them.

I could identify as I had a Harmony/Granny in South Korea. I just thought I could identify with wanting to be be like everyone else in America's version of beauty and Americanness. Beverly Hillbillies was about a dirt poor family that struck it rich, didn't have a fancy education, but just tried to be neighborly and kind simple folk values. The plot line is that people tried to take advantage of them, but it all worked out in the end.

Now that I think about it extended family, moved clear across the country, yep I learned manners and the differences in class and societal polish. I'm a quick study and I learned to adapt to whatever came my way. I was a social chameleon in that I was able to be with everyone. Originally when I came to America, I lived in a very small town 675 in Florence, Texas.

Thank goodness, I lived in such a small town, because people were kind and helpful. We also had two teachers in the Kindergarten-2nd grade. That was how I learned to read and excel in the basics, because we had blue birds which were the fastest readers, red birds were second, green birds third and yellow birds were the slowest readers in First grade. We had 20 students in my grade. So between, television, reading my books and my brother's books, I became an avid speed reader.

My brother, Jin bought a bicycle from delivering The Austin American Statesman and Sundays were our favorite because of The Comics. This town was more Mayberry in the Andy Griffith Show. The town had its characters, but everyone was neighborly. I also was an honorary cub scout, because we were latch key kids, my adoptive dad would have tours in Vietnam and my adoptive mom worked at a nursing home and she would get home at 11 pm. Jin and I would do our homework, then we watched tv and we loved Mission Impossible and would turn off the tv and scurry off to bed before she got out of the car. She probably knew we had been up, but she never said anything. Probably because we had good grades.

I had a hard time moving to Lampasas, population 5,725 in 1970 for 3rd Grade out in the country. Before, my brother and I had such freedom because he would bike and I would ride on the crossbar all throughout town. So he was in cub scouts and they let me be an honorary member. In Lampasas, we were too young to drive and it was far to a neighbor. Also I was the new girl, I had a boy's haircut and ugly cat rim glasses. Everyone was already best friends with people from Kindergarten and I looked and felt like an outsider.

Also 3rd grade, we actually traded classes for homeroom and then we had different subjects. I was used to getting additional help if I needed and now I was in a class of 23 kids with only one teacher. Math was my nemesis as this is when you learn multiplication. I kept bombing my tests. Until one day I understood Multiplication vs. Addition. I finally had a lightbulb moment and it clicked, but it was well into the second quarter. So I was considered dumb on math but way ahead on my reading SRA. I was shy, but I tried to make friends and I became friends with a teacher's daughter and her friends. I even got to go to sleepover once.

My aunt/adoptive mom was frugal and so she made our clothes from fabric that was on sale. So I was dressed in hand me downs from my brother and whatever she made. I was definitely in an ugly duckling phase of my life. By the 5th grade, my clothes got better and by the 6th grade I started making money babysitting and I bought my own clothes. I never looked back to how ugly and unworthy, I felt because I understood I could be attractive with the right clothes and makeup. I developed earlier than everyone else. I was taller than a lot of boys too. I am so glad that stage of development and growth is over.

I tell people I learned English and mannerisms from the television mostly and I would observe people I wanted to emulate. Adam 12, Mission Impossible, Captain Kangaroo and the local Uncle Jay's Show.

I also watched the Carol Burnett Show, Smothers Brothers, Laugh In, Hee Haw, Porter Wagner's Show and The Lawrence Welk Show.. There were very little representation of an Asian American, much less black people unless it was degrading servants or exaggerated buck teeth and glasses like Breakfast at Tiffany's. Much as I love that movie, I hate that Japanese neighbor story line. As it was such an over the top caricature of a bumbling idiot and accent.

As a Korean American, growing up in small towns in Texas, I had to correct people from thinking I was Chinese or Japanese American, but a Korean American. I was so happy when MASH the tv show came out. At least I could say I'm Korean American and people did know we were in a war there too before Vietnam.

There were a few times when racism was overt like a fight in which a girl threatened to hit me in 7th Grade and called me, "A slant-eyed bitch!" But it was more like in Oklahoma people thought I was Indian (native American) or in Indiana when my boyfriend's little boy next door asked, "Are you from Hawaii?" However in Texas, it was more like my best friend, Laura and I went to my Presbyterian Church in Lampasas where a sweet old lady just labeled us, "one of those people." We weren't sure whether she meant Mexican or Korean, because we look nothing alike.

It's the sense of otherness, that you feel. I tell people in Texas, it was Hierarchy of Whiteness or Lightness or Colorism from Colonialism. Having traveled all around the world, I can attest to this subtle and sometimes not so subtle discrimination. As I clearly have an American accent, people aren't quite as discriminatory as they are with my immigrant family that may have a slightly different English than them.

In Indiiana, my sister and I were at the Carmel Methodist Church and an elderly parishioner came up to me and said, "I understand you so much better than that lady," pointing to my sister. My sister was pretty outraged as she had been teaching in Indiana University for several years and been speaking English in America for over 16 years in academia.

In September of 2016, my sons and I went to Leesburg Premium Outlet on Labor Day Weekend to shop for back to school deals on clothes and shoes. I thought it was a very American thing as I have been doing it ever since I had children going back to school. We are even told this in advertising and unlike the 60's and 70's. There are diverse races and models in ads, movies and television shows of diversity in America. While it's still not super white anymore, you can find whiteness programming on the Hallmark Channel. Almost everywhere else there is still preponderance of white people, we can say there are Asians besides MASH.

Like so many Asian Americans and I mean people from the Middle East, India, Indonesia, Thailand, Vietnamese, Koreans, Taiwanese, Japanese and Chinese descent were there as were Hispanics, Latinos, white and black Americans all doing their back to school rite of passage. When my boys and I were passing a white couple coming out of Michael Kors store loudly, the male said, "It's Chinatown Here!" I remember staring at him and like wanting to turn around and Cameron, my 16 year old son says, "Mom don't!" He knew I was going to go and confront the guy. I was going to say, "Excuse me, but I'm a Korean American here and there are many different Asian Americans shopping here too, not just Chinese!"

I didn't get to confront him, but I did ask Cameron if that comment bothered him and he shrugs, "No!" I remember my Facebook post about this and some of the feedback from what I called Woke Folks! We got it that this is code for these people aren't Americans pursuing the American Dream of consumerism. These people are foreigners taking our jobs and taking exceptionalism and meritocracy on its head. We are the silent Asians that are in this limbo of looking visibly different but feeling the same model minority American. I've spent 53 years in America and now I have a President that says, " Go back to where you're from!" On July 14, 2019, Trump tells the Squad this coded language of White Supremacy, "Go back where you're from!" Three of the four were born in America, only Ilhan Omar was an immigrant like me as a child. +

That brought up old suppressed feeling of not enoughness, that a child already gets as an immigrant adoptee by a white racist pedophile dad married to your Korean maternal aunt. This is why I knew that tiny microaggression of September 2016 would lead to a US President saying that on live television and tweeting proudly about it. Having Fox Television saying, "That's not racist!" This the years of being told as a child, "Koreans are lazy!" That "Kimchi and Korean food stink!" "Koreans stink!" "Koreans are dumb!" These were some of the things I heard from my adoptive dad from 4 ½ to almost 11 years old. Or as my testimony for the Montgomery County Council when I was speaking on child maltreatment speaking on funding: the feelings of shame, blame, guilt and humiliation can be retriggered throughout your life.

I'm glad Cameron can just brush off a remark like that because he has had to deal with less racism than I did. His childhood was in Fairfax and Herndon in Fairfax County, VA and Gaithersburg in Montgomery County, MD. We deliberately lived in a diverse metro area with an international flair that is very different from NYC, but I felt was less disparity in income. It's why I came to this area to make America better.

During the past almost 5 ½ years, we went from "Mexicans are rapists!" to Muslim Ban, caged children in Family Separation Act, After the White Supremacist rally in Charlottesville, VA, "There are very fine people on both sides!"

But that's the thing, I may wear American clothes, but because my facial features are Asian, I am more likely to be told, "Go back to your Country!" Like President Trump told the Squad on July 14, 2019, "Go back to where you came from!" To Representatives Alexandria O'Casio, Illhan Omar, Rashid Taalib and Ayana Pressley! That was one night that I watched Fox commentators gaslight my experience of the comment, "Go back to where you're from!" In the 70's and 80's, it was, "Go back to your country!" When Vietnamese fisherman were trying to fish in the Gulf of Mexico. I was in Texas and remember those slights.

Now I've got to worry that my friends that have green cards can't get CoVid-19 stimulus $1200 checks nor their American citizen spouse, even while they are paying US taxes. As a model minority, people don't want to make waves and there's a difference sometimes. I've got to combat and fight for CoVid19 aid for our Sanctuary County, because Trump wants to punish Blue States. It's war and I feel traumatized like my childhood reading under the covers with a flashlight in my bed. I was too scared to go to sleep and it was so much safer in my stories that I read in my books. While I try to escape in a good romance book, I know unlike the book, as an adult, life in America may not have a happy ending! However, I will do everything I can to make America and the world a better place!

Embarassing Moments

On Facebook, my girlfriend Lily Liu challenges me to write about my assimilation experiences.

Lily Liu, in the spirit of your lead, I will write about my Oma's resourcefulness under Japanese occupation in Korea, resourcefulness that she brought with her to America. My Oma is a forager of immense knowledge. When she came to the US in 1972, she gathered spring greens, dandelions and oak acorns in Lampasas, Texas.

Much to my embarrassment and humiliation, my parents would gather acorns at the park near the river. They would gather bags and my Obigie would bicycle these bags back home. They would shell the acorns and soak them to get rid of the bitterness. Then they would dry them in the sun. Then they created an industrial strength mortar and pestle out of a cemented pail and a hand-carved post. With it, they made mook, an acorn jelly, and sold it to Asian grocery stores.

My parents used that same mortar and pestle, twice a week, to make rice powder for rice cakes. My Oma grew Korean peppers, squash, Korean melons, sesame seeds, Chinese cabbage, onions and herbs. That was how they sent my sister and her husband through collage; my sister went all the way to get her PhD. That garden and Korean prepared foods like kimchi, rice cakes, steamed buns and mook also paid for my sister's lifestyle in Austin.

In the 90's, I worked in Georgetown and had a massage studio on 29th street. My parents would come to work with me and go and pick gingko nuts nearby. Gingko fruit smells like rotten eggs and so did my parents because the gingko got on their shoes. I would drive them home at the end of the day. Sometimes, if they weren't ready to leave, I would quickly fill their bag with ginko so we could go.

It was quite a process getting my parents, and their ginko, in the car. We put extra plastic bags around our shoes so we wouldn't spread the mushy, sulphur, rotten egg-smelling fruit. I also lined the trunk of the car with big black trash bags. Once home, my parents would wash off the smelly fruit.

My Oma has spent more years in America than Korea and says proudly, "I am American!" I answer, "Yes, you are an American so vote out Trump in six months!" That is my goal for my Oma. She already made it to another goal: her 92nd birthday. She reached that milestone just before the pandemic and we celebrated it at her Korean church along with my brother, Jin. My older sister and brother couldn't be bothered to make it to the occasion of celebrating her living birthday. My Asian family values have been adopted by my sons and hubby; we honor our elders and we take turns in watching my Oma. It definitely takes a committed family to keep from institutionalizing parents and I am proud of the way our family has made the choices we have made together. I have also told my sons, I do not expect this from them.

Now I am proud of my parents for being frugal and resourceful, but back then I was worried about what others thought and whether I would be humiliated by my classmates. Now, I own that I was different and I am proud to have the resiliency of spirit and the bravery to make it in America!

Forgiveness Prayers

Thanks to Howard Wills (via Mirabai Devi)

Below is the link to the Howard Wills prayer site. I am including my original introduction to his work when I was being coached on Inner Alignment and became certified as an Inner Alignment Coach. Thank you, Kimberly Beekman for deepening my Forgiveness Practice and knowing the healing and freedom of the power of forgiveness. It frees oneself from the poison of holding onto the hurt and righteousness of being wronged. Instead it allows one to choose to move on with the lesson and wisdom while letting go of the pain. I appreciate gratitude, grace and forgiveness as the cornerstones of my recovery and healing. This is just to pass on what has helped me to accept my own power to choose Love over Fear.

https://howardwills.com/prayers

General Forgiveness Prayer

"I forgive you. Please forgive me. Let's forgive ourselves. Please Divine, Thank you Divine. Amen"

OR

"I release you. Please release me. Let's release ourselves. Please Divine, Thank you Divine. Amen"

A longer prayer from Howard (and Mirabai)

"[Person's name], I forgive you for all the ways that you have hurt me, physically, emotionally, mentally, psychically, spiritually, sexually, financially, or in any other way, knowingly or unknowingly, in the past, present, or future through thought, word, or deed; through [words to describe their negative words or actions and to describe your feelings about this person's negative words and actions], please forgive me for all of the ways in which I have hurt you, physically, emotionally, mentally, psychically, spiritually, sexually, financially, or in any other way, knowingly or unknowingly, through thought, word, or deed, through [words to describe your negative words or actions toward them]. Divine, please help [person's name] and me to forgive each other and to forgive ourselves. Please, Divine. Thank you, Divine. Amen."

Ho'oponpono Prayer from Hawaii

"I love you, I'm sorry, Please forgive me, Thank you."

Family Lineage Forgiveness Prayers

Prayer to cleanse relationships with all women (left side of upper body and right leg):

"For all of the women who have ever hurt me, I forgive you, all of you. Mother(s), mother-inlaw(s), daughter(s), daughter(s)-in-law, sister(s), sister(s)- in-law, aunt(s), grandmothers, friends, ex-lover(s)/ex-wife(s), partner(s), wife. I ask that you all please forgive me. Divine Light, please help us all to forgive each other and to forgive ourselves. Let us all forgive and release ourselves for our hurts, wrongs, and mistakes to ourselves and to others. Please, Divine Light. Thank you, Divine Light. Amen"

Prayer to cleanse relationships with all men (right side of upper body and left leg):

"For all of the men who have ever hurt me, I forgive you, all of you. Father(s), father(s)-inlaw, son(s), son(s)-in-law, brother(s), brother(s)-in-law, uncle(s), grandfathers, friends, exlover(s)/ex-husband(s), partner(s), husband. I ask that you all please forgive me. Divine Light, please help us all to forgive each other and to forgive ourselves. Let us all forgive and release ourselves for our hurts, wrongs, and mistakes to ourselves and to others. Please, Divine Light. Thank you, Divine Light. Amen"

Another Lineage Forgiveness Prayer

"Divine, for me and my entire lineage throughout all time, past, present, and future: please help us all forgive all people, help all people forgive us, and help us all forgive ourselves. Please, Divine. Thank you, Divine. Amen"

Full Power Prayer

"Divine, please help me forgive all people, help all people forgive me, and help us all forgive ourselves. Please Divine, Thank you.

Divine, for me and my entire lineage, throughout all time, past present, and future: Please help us all forgive all people, help all people forgive us, and help us all forgive ourselves. Please Divine, Thank you.

Divine, for me, my spouse(s), all our family members, all our relationships, all our ancestors, and all relationship with all creations and life forms, throughout all time, past present, and future: Please help us all forgive all people, help all people forgive us, and help us all forgive ourselves. Completely and totally. Please Divine, Thank you.

Divine, please help us all love each other and love ourselves, be at peace with each other and be at peace with ourselves. Please Divine, Thank you.

Divine, we give you our love and thank you for your constant love and blessings. We love and appreciate all your creations, and we fill your creations with our love. We love you Divine. Thank you for loving us. We love you Divine. Thank you for loving us. We love you Divine. Thank you for loving us. Thank You Divine, Amen.

Divine, please open, bless, empower, expand, lead, guide, direct and protect me, my family, all humanity and all of creation, throughout all time, now and forever. Please Divine, thank you Divine. Amen."

Self-forgiveness

"[Self], I forgive you for all the ways you have hurt me, through [list all the ways you've hurt yourself]. Divine, please help me to forgive myself and to be forgiven for all of my mistakes, hurts, and wrongs to myself and to others. Please Divine, thank you Divine. Amen"

OR

Another from G. R. King's St. Germain book series: "Divine, release me from every mistake I've ever made, and replace those mistakes by such Ascended Master Sacred Fire Blessing and Perfection and Happiness to the rest of life that I never think of them again. They can never be existing anywhere in the Universe and no one else can be touched by them!"

Critical Race Theory is not Anti-Asian

March 22, 2021 by Mari Matsuda

This is so important as I have been a Progressive Asian American Christian Fellowship from August of 2020 and will graduate in June 2021. I've been in deep dive of Asian American history against the backdrop of European and American Colonialism.

We have looked into racism, sexism, disability justice and identities. We studied this intersectionality of internment camps, Yuri Kochiyama, Malcolm X and unjust imprisonment of black and brown Brothers and sisters. I have deeply dived into the White Male Privilege of Christianity and until 50 years ago there were very rare incidents of Asian American Christian scholars.

I have looked into the question of whether the Middle East is part of Asia and in my mind, yes. I dated my college sweetheart who was Jewish at 18. I had to examine my own anti Semitism bias and beliefs. I took a comparative World Religions class. My female professor in 1981 was pretty radical white woman deeply immersed in the Vedic tradition of Hinduism.

I got to experience and opened my heart and mind to the truth of most religions evolved to give guidelines to live a "good life" within a society of generosity, gratitude, caring for self and others, forgiving self and others, loving self and others, having a connection to Source, Nature, God, Goddess, Force, Universe, Light or Higher Power. So yes, I believe all people are my fellow brothers and sisters. I have been actively progressing human and environmental rights since I was 18 and I am turning 59 in May. I believe in a world where there are no more "Throw-Away People" and a sustainable world that works in harmony and appreciation of Planet Earth. Hugs and blessings on a most beautiful Sunday!

http://reappropriate.co/2021/03/mari-matsuda-critical-race-theory-is-not-anti-asian/

As a Survivor of Child Sexual Abuse

As a Survivor of Child Sexual Abuse, I understand the shame, blame, guilt and humiliation that comes with going public. My adoptive mom asked me at 12 if anything had happened sexually with my adoptive dad. I told her the truth, yes, every night and especially on Saturdays. She said, "If it happens again, it's your fault!" It continued to happen again and I was burdened with the shame of several lifetimes of my adoptive parents and my first family.

I was told to not speak of it again as, "It brings shame to our family!" That's the part of our rape culture is to make it unsafe to speak out because of the blaming, shaming, and guilting along with public humiliation. That's why people have kept it buried all these years. I have so many friends and peers that have never reported their rapes or sexual assaults because they were and are afraid to be looked at differently. I understand this, as it was shameful for me throughout so much of my childhood and early adulthood.

I also know once I have disclosed my own history of childhood rape, women and men have disclosed to me their own occurrence of rape. Many times, I'm the first that they have disclosed their secret to and many times, they're able to let go of so much of the pain, shame, blame, guilt and fear they carry around for a lifetime. I'm speaking out because it happens across all cultures, races, religions and economic classes. One in four girls will experience some type of sexual assault before the age of 18. I create the space for safety and compassion. I am continuing to do this so people know they are believed and cared for and I will say, "I'm sorry you experienced this in your life. I believe you! On behalf of the Universe, I want to apologize from the Universe! (Thank you, Robin Rice for giving me this piece in healing and acceptance).

I chose to publish my story three years ago to coincide with Asian

American Pacific Islanders Heritage Month. It was a few months ahead of the second wave of #MeToo originally started by Tarana Burke in 2006. Women and girls of color have even bigger hurdles to overcome to find their voice.

People ask me how I am able to bare my soul's wounds so publicly, and I tell them, I hit my 50's. At 50, I say, "My BS meter is quick and I realized I don't have time to deal with BS." I DO SPEAK TRUTH even when it's not convenient. I realize that's part of my soul's mission is to advocate and empower those who are marginalized and unable to speak up for their rights. The most empowering way to live my life is to give meaning in a way that empowers me. I have a choice to continue to write my story of impact and meaning because I let go of my attachment to what others think about me. I realize I am enough and I will always speak my truth to make the greatest impact in my community and world. I chose not to live in the past but focus on how I can live my best life with my friends and family. I am grateful for all the touchpoints of community and caring. I also believe that Love and Compassion to create Joy and Peace in our world is my lifelong purpose.

Hugs and blessings from the #MeToo and #MeTooCSA front lines.

Asia 1989, Part 1

In summer of 1989, I made a very life affirming trip to NYC, Japan and Korea. I went and visited NYC first because there was a reticence to actually go to Korea, my homeland. I went for 4 weeks and finally bought my ticket to Korea from JFK via Tokyo. I didn't have a lot of money and knew Tokyo was very expensive, but thought my 7 hour layover in Tokyo Narita Airport could be fun. I figured I would have a two hour tour of Tokyo and go onto Seoul's Kimpo Airport.

The travails of international travel then vs. now. I had met a friend of a friend in NYC that had a friend in Tokyo and gave me his number in case I had a chance to look him up. Needless to say the best laid plans of arriving in Tokyo at 2 pm and making my connection to Seoul at 9 pm, didn't happen because United Airlines had a bad computer chip. My flight was delayed for 11 hours while they waited for the Tokyo to JFK plane to arrive so they could switch chips. I ended up in Tokyo at 9 pm with no help for hotels. I was left to my own resources with just a voucher for plane travel not a hotel voucher.

I ended up calling my contact in Tokyo phone number and couldn't understand them Japanese vs. English, but I thought the only other language I knew was Spanish. Turns out that was their other language. I got the correct phone number to call in Tokyo at Yomiuri Shinbun, a workplace for my contact. I end up calling and explaining my situation and he was gracious enough to explain how to get to Tokyo on the Airport Limousine Bus and asked me how he would recognize me as he was wearing a lavender tie. I answered, "I have long black hair and I'm Oriental." He was stunned and said, "Do you know where you are?" It was my first time since I left Korea in 1967 to be in a country where I looked like the majority of people.

My frame of reference for myself and what made me stand out from the crowd no longer worked in a land of Asians. All my paradigms no longer worked and I learned an important lesson about being part of the majority vs. minority population. We both laughed and I told him I was wearing a black skirt with a denim jacket with a painted back of me and lots of pins. The kindness of strangers when you travel was never as important as it was that night.

I've spoken about this trip and this incident, but I am writing about this as our country puts up so many barriers to people who want to visit and experience America and juxtapose this hostile and unkind fashion vs. the kindness of strangers in a strange land helping a stranded traveler out. The Good Samaritan Parable or the Golden Rule are good examples in the Old and New Testaments of the Bible. That's why when I see tourists in Washington, DC lost I try to help them navigate to their destination.

I also try to be kind to anyone with an accent in their English as I know they have been brave to come here and a little kindness takes nothing financially, but expands humanity and resilience. Hugs and blessings from my tales of a life well lived and loved!

Asia 1989, Part 2

This is my next part of my story of my Tokyo excursion in 1989. My contact in Tokyo was a journalist for Yomiuri Shinbun. After my phone call with my AHA moment of I'm no longer in America, I get on the Airport Limousine Bus for Tokyo. Takao meets me and recognizes me from all my political buttons, including my ironic "I don't speak English button!" Which he gets a laugh out of that pin in particular. He pays for a taxi because I have a really big bag having to retrieve my checked on International luggage.

His apartment is in Kawasaki city. He shows me really interesting technology in his on-demand water heater, the bathroom amenities, bidet and the air conditioner was tiny. He helps me set up my tatami mat with bedding futon and I had some tea and ramen. He had gotten a Master's in Journalism in Chicago and learned to speak English during his time in the States. His beat was making sense of American politics and Reagan.so we ended up talking about Reagan's kitchen Cabinet as it was well understood, Reagan was suffering from dementia.

The next morning, I finish folding up my bedding and get ready to go sightseeing in Tokyo including Tokyo Tower and I get a big Japanese yellow button to add to my collection of pins. We also get to see the palace park in Tokyo and have lunch before I get back on Airport Limousine Bus back to Narita. He gives me his contact and friend in Seoul and invites me back to visit on my return trip. Since, I have my plane voucher, I agree to come back in a month after my Korea visit.

I fly into Kimpo Airport and as I disembark, my sister, my niece and my parents are there to greet me at my gate. My niece even had a welcome sign with my name. This was my first time back home since I was adopted at 3 YO and left as a 4 YO. I am grateful that I got to experience this coming home since I left Korea in 1967 after being adopted. So 22 years later at 27, I really am welcomed home by my biological family. During this time in Seoul, I get to meet my Obigie's relatives and see the tiny house that I lived in Inchon. I even asked the current owners to let me see my childhood home. It was tiny and I took pictures. I also met the midwife that delivered me as a footling breach baby and saved both my Oma's and my life during my birth. It was a reclaiming of my identity as both a South Korean and as an American.

I learned more about history, Korean modern art and fashion during that trip. I also learned Korea had the first printing press 100 years ahead of Guttenberg. Because we had a wise King that created Hangul language for children and women to become literate instead of the pictograms of the Chinese characters. After hosting the Summer Olympics of 1988, Korea was beginning to show its Economic muscle. I got to experience Korean food and ended up meeting the Japanese journalist and his wife for dinner at Lotte Restaurant. There I was given the contact info of his parents and an Invitation to stay at his parents' home, when I visited Tokyo on my way back.

I was and am fortunate that people do like me enough to go out of their way to be kind. After my month in Seoul of sightseeing, I end up visiting Japan for another two weeks and end up with a Japanese boyfriend. My rebellion from my parents, I decided to date my Japanese friend. As there are definitely major issues between my parents' generation that experienced Japanese occupation and my generation that did not. I learned rudimentary Japanese and how to navigate the subway and train system of Tokyo and suburbs. It's actually easy to navigate once you learn the difference between express and local lines.

1989 and 1990 were my years of coming to peace about being an Asian American and I did my senior thesis on Eastern and Western Thought. I wrote that I wanted to be the Bridge between East and West. I wrote about Quantum physics and how they were using Eastern philosophies to explain reality. During this time, I realized I'm an American in my beliefs and values of government and justice. I came to Washington, DC armed with my Political Science degree and thought I would change the world politically. Instead I became a Healer that eventually learned to heal myself and others.

India 1994, Part 1: Gratitude

I'm going to regale you with my month long trip to India in January of 1994. I always credit India for allowing me to learn Gratitude in my bones and learning my true worth. My boyfriend and I went to India to visit his friend in New Delhi and to travel the country ending with a stay at Guru Mai outside Mumbai. As with all things, best laid plans change.

We end up flying to Frankfurt Airport from Baltimore, MD with a pretty significant layover and end up partying in the airport with German friends that came into the airport to meet us. Those were the days when you could actually enter airports and meet people at the gates upon arrival. Anyway we had a great time drinking German wine and eating sausages catching up on friendships for 5 hours. Then we get on another flight to New Delhi which was another 11 hour flight after the already 9 hour flight. So we arrive at 11 pm New Delhi time. At that time the airport was pretty deserted except for our flight. Our friend meets us and we get our luggage and go to our friend's house. We're quite tired but it's exciting to be in India and know that we are in an enclave of expats and foreign nationals residential community. There's steady electricity and water and doesn't seem too different from what you're used to as an American. The furniture and textiles of course are different. But we settle in for the night.

The next morning we are given a mango, papaya and yogurt breakfast with freshly squeezed orange juice. My very favorite breakfast in India. The fruits were incredibly sweet because it was local and picked at peak freshness. We went out to see shops as I needed personal care items and we were going to sandalwood carvers. We end up going to the government run shops/ artisans and pick up a beautiful Lakshmi. On the car ride to the shops I saw such heartbreaking vignettes of poverty, child malnutrition and labor. Plus because we wore Western garb, we were mobbed by the begging children and we could see the adult in the background that ran the circle of beggars.

If you don't know that I am an Intuitive Empath Healer, so literally I am being bombarded by desperation and hunger pains. It's overwhelming and I am recoiling almost into a ball. My boyfriend and his friend help me into the car and we speed away. I'm literally crying as I can't help myself from being awash in all this pain. The guys are thinking it's my PMS, but I explain I'm overwhelmed by the smells, oversensory stimulation and my sensitivity to the plight and suffering I experienced. The guys let me go off to take a nap.

I end up crying and experiencing my dark night of the soul moment because I am in such physical and emotional pain. I had an epiphany of I can allow myself to be overwhelmed by it or just feel extreme gratitude for my privileged life. Up until that point, I still would flip into my victimhood. This I realized was a choice and I needed to make my most empowering choice in my framework. From this moment, I realized while I had a shitty childhood, I didn't worry about food or shelter. I could work towards making life better for all people or I could be in misery about my own pain.

That was when I chose to rewrite my life story as having a crappy childhood, but having an amazing adulthood filled with travel and experiences with people with wealth and privilege. My hubby and I talk about it's the stories you tell yourself and others that make up your life. So I teach storytelling for Survivors to Thrivers. This was my other AHA moment. My Inda trip taught me profound gratitude for what is and simultaneously knowing that I am Healing, I am Healed and I am a Healer! Hugs and blessings! I hope you are benefitting from my travel AHA moments that created the person I am today with strength and resilience because of my gratitude and responses to life!

India 1994, Part 2: Triangle

Continuing my 1994 India tales. My boyfriend's friend worked for the German Degussa now Evonik corporation. Just outside New Delhi is their silicon dioxide plant which harvests beautiful white sand for a raw material needed throughout manufacturing. We are honored guests and learn a lot about the Brahman class because of the employees that are there. We're able to eat one of my most memorable vegetarian meals was chestnut stuffed potatoes and many curries and dahl along with naan.

Being friends with the Executive, we were given tours of the processing plant. We also planted ashoka trees, one with my boyfriend's name and my own tree that I planted with the gardener with it's own plaque with my name and date. This tree is revered for its beauty and fast growth and known as a success tree as well as a reason to return to India. This was also my first day to just be in reverence and gratitude to help me deal with the overwhelming barrage of great wealth and poverty within the same blocks. I'm sure a lot of this has changed. In 1994, India was a third world country that had the largest middle class in the world. At this time, my observation was amazement at the disparities of wealth and poverty.

My observations at the time was that I was surprised that people accepted their fate in the society that I observed in the two different servants of the household. One was the driver and the other was more like the butler. There was a power struggle where the driver was kicked out of the house. I remember thinking that the driver's life would get worse, because he lived an hour away and his day started early in the morning and ended late at night. Whereas there was the color of the skin and the caste system at play. The lighter skinned guy made our food and had different sales people come by to sell us silk knotted rugs and other textiles. I'm sure he also got a commission on our purchases.

We took a tour of the golden triangle which is the New Dehli, the Bahai Lotus Temple which at that time was the cleanest attraction that we went to in India. There's ritual in taking off your shoes and experiencing the tranquility and sacredness of space. We went to other temples that were more Hindu and bought the marigold necklaces and were given the red third eye mark. I didn't drink from the Ganges River but I did go to its banks. In some ways, now I wish I had bathed in the River, but at the time, I didn't want to get dirty going into the river.

We went to the Fatehpur Sikri or the Red Fort that had no source of water inside but was where the ruler that built the Taj Mahal was imprisoned and he had a special convex mirror that he was able to see his wife's tomb. Such beauty and tragedy. We stayed the night in Agra at an Indian Hotel and my boyfriend got some custom tailored shirts. I got two saris, one made of teal silk with a matching beaded and embroidered jacket with a fuschia top. Plus a a black sari with fuschia, gold, green accents with a different fuschia top. There was a buffet and I tried all kinds of dishes, but butter chicken was my favorite dish. We got to see the Taj Mahal at night driving by and from our hotel.

In the morning, we approached the Taj Mahal and had the traditional picture sitting on the bench in front. At that time there were many of the carnelian, lapis and other semi precious stones missing throughout the Taj Mahal. It was beautiful but definitely showing the wear of being a tourist attraction where people took pieces of it home. There were stone carvers outside that also would sell souvenirs of white marble pieces mimicking the Taj Mahal inlays. At the time, there was talk of restoration, but it had not happened yet. Agra was a beautiful tourist city and very used to tourists.

Throughout these excursions we did have an English speaking tour guide that also takes you to different vendors. We also went to Jaipur which has pink roofs since 1875 for Prince Albert and Queen Victoria's visit. It's quite a picturesque city and there were museums we went to as well as shopping. We made it back to New Dehli to sleep before we embarked on our more exotic excursions.

We get up fairly early and get to the airport to go to Khajuraho which is out of the way. At the airport, there were tiny Catholic schoolgirls flying to some other destination and they end up coming up to me to talk. I remember one particular girl gave me a 5 rupee note and I gave her my American change and a dollar. It was delightful to be asked so many questions of where I'm from because I'm an American from Korea. We flew Air India because that was the only airline in India. At that time it was literally held together with duct tape. More on this later.

Khajuraho is a most magical place in that there are beautiful Hindu and Jain temples. It has the most beautiful natural stone formations and home of the Kama Sutra temples. The Jain and Zorastrians were what I remember most about this area. This was the least populated area that we visited and had beautiful deserted and crumbling structures. One of the reasons it wasn't destroyed by Muslims was that a forest had overgrown the area and protected it for centuries. We saw rock canyons and just incredible natural beauty. This was the most healing of the places we visited because of its natural scenic beauty and I got to hug my trees. We were there for two days visiting with a driver and a tour guide. This was my favorite area because I wasn't inundated with begging children and didn't see lame people with missing limbs.

I hope you are enjoying my travelogues from my memories. Hugs and blessings until tomorrow when I will cover Udaipur.

India 1994, Part 3: Self Worth

Today is how I realized my own worth and value in India in 1994 in New Dehli. My boyfriend was 20 years my senior and already had a son from a previous marriage. He really wanted a play partner not a growth partner. We had already had a 2 week trip to Germany where I found black patent Birkenstocks with small straps and lavender soles and a pink, lavender and aqua buckles and fell in love with German shoes. During Oktoberfest which is in September of 1993 and we had a great time in a first world country touring wineries and festivals along with scenic and romantic dinners in renovated castles, cruises along the Rhine River.

I had even quit working at the Four Seasons as an employee and was a contractor as a massage therapist so I could take the month vacation. While he loved me and I loved him, it became apparent our values and political beliefs would be at odds in a Third World country like India. While I had been in Mexico, it was not as crowded nor as desperately poor as India. He wanted to have a great time shopping, traveling and dining like before. I couldn't be as happy go lucky as I was in Germany. Because I was faced with such injustice and inequality of such magnitude, I couldn't just ignore this in my heart. I wanted to save the children and the women. But I didn't have enough personal wealth to save them. This was where I learned to acknowledge everyone with Namaste and to learn reverence and acknowledgement.

This was also where we both went to the Tibetan store in New Delhi and this was where I spent my own money buying a pantsuit sets in greenish black and burgundy and my Om Mani Padme Om silver cuff bracelet. Unfortunately the quality of the Tibetan wares were not very good on the silver. The pantsuit was extremely comfortable and wore well. I kept the green one and gave my sister the burgundy set. While it was a blend, it looked like raw silk in the nubby texture. I also bought a lot of textiles wanting to support the Dalai Lama and exiled Tibetans. I ended up speaking to the manager of the store saying I was an American and wanted to continue to support this cause. Nothing came of it other than I spent what money I had at this store and came back to see how I could further the mission.

We also went to Mother Theresa's orphanage in New Delhi. We went and toured the facility and played with the children. It was interesting to experience an orphanage as an adoptee. At the time I remember thinking it was very clean and the children were cared for by older children and young women. Now I have much more mixed feelings about this as it's a charity that has brought her worldwide fame and accolades. But as a Survivor, there are definitely both sides that I see.

We went to art museums where I was astonished at the many workers that were gambling instead of really tending the landscapes around the museums. I kept thinking there was such waste of resources not keeping things clean and pristine for tourists and visitors. Instead they were whiling their time away playing games of chance. It was definitely my Western mind and values, but there were lots of things in disrepair and lots of labor, but not the end results that I would have expected. I knew there were some very hardworking Indians and then the caste system seemed at play here.

I also experienced an Indian call center and a programming company. I'm sad that I didn't stay in touch with some of the programmers. We had gone to meet my boyfriend's friend's girlfriend at her work. He also was the same age as my boyfriend and his girlfriend was also 23 years younger. He had already bought her a car and helped with her parents because he loved her so much. He also had kids and an ex- wife. But he was getting ready to marry her in a year and his children had already met her and were happy. We went and got the other under skirts for my saris and I learned how to fold and wrap my teal beaded and embroidered silk sari and jacket.

We took our elegantly dressed selves to a very posh Indian 5 star hotel in New Delhi and after eating shopped in the promenade area. I bought 3 sets of handcrafted puppets a man and wife sets for my two nieces and nephews. Plus two more sets for us. This was our last evening before my boyfriend would go to Eat Pray Love at Guru Mai's ashram. He was excited and dissatisfied that I wouldn't go with him to Mumbai/ Bombay. But I had said, "That's it! I'm not flying Air India!" So he went off to Mumbai and I stayed in New Delhi with his friend we got to socialize with his girlfriend at night. During the day his driver would take him to his work and come back for me and took me back to Tibetan Center and other Buddhist sites and different interesting temples.

On one of the trips to pick up the friend from Degussa, we saw the huge Indian Vultures on the side of the road. These birds scared me how big they are and they are going extinct because of poisons now. They were majestic and scary in a fog laden area next to the road. It was during these trips we got to learn more about each other's lives. It was these heart to heart talks that I said that I didn't think his friend, my boyfriend loved me enough to be about my happiness. I would need to be all about being a fun companion, but in 20 years I would be taking care of an old man without experiencing the first of life together like buying a house and having children.

He was very clear he wanted to get married, but no children. His friend was very realistic and wanted to have children with his fiancee. Because he wanted her first experiences of marriage and children and to experience it all with her. By the time my boyfriend returned a week later, I realized my interests and values were at odds with his values and wants. I realize now why I haven't touched Indira Gandhi's books. I did read them and that's why I haven't touched them since.

My boyfriend came back excited because he got to see Guru Mai as he gave free dental services for some of her staff in the States in the NY ashram and so he was given differential treatment. He enjoyed the time and was ready to enjoy the physical pleasures of life again. He got to check his box that he was meditating and he was ready to resume life as normal. They say travel changes you as you find new strengths and skills of resourcefulness. In India, your openness and kindness matters. I guess through gratitude I received Grace.

We tried to work on our relationship, but my blinders of love had come off on at that time my hardest trip of my life. But now I can say China in 2013 was my hardest trip. Until next time, Namaste!

This Too Shall Pass

"And this too shall pass," was and is still my favorite parenting mantra to make it to the next moment. Much like this global reset because of a global pandemic, my family and I are making decisions daily about keeping ourselves, extended family and friends under our circle of care.

Change is usually created by Trauma or Illness; it makes one examine priorities instead of sleep walking through the plans established by society, parents and other influences. Change is an opportunity to figure out what affirms your energy and life force. I call these emotions everything that includes courage so you are living with your own truth; there's a reason we and psychology call them life-changing moments.

Courage is literally willing to live, love and forgive as life continues to unfold. We can grow and embrace life with love, laughter and grace or we can shrink as we try to worry and control everything. I say there's a balance in taking in society's well-being as well as my own. We are seeing it all unfold and our shadow traits are showing up in news feeds from a US President and from people spewing fear and hatred. The only path forward is a time out and to hold reconciliation meetings. When I cannot see myself in another human being, my skill as an empath will be gone, as I will have discarded a piece of my own humanity.

We are all equal and I will always stand for equality, justice and freedom. I hope that we can have a peaceful transfer of power, but I am also realistic in realizing how complicit our government can be in maintaining the status quo. While I pray for a peaceful transition of power in free and fair elections I am also realistic when it comes to the US Senate and Supreme Court enabling this Administration to continue to stay in power.

I may be wrong about what can transpire in the next six months in the midst of a global pandemic with an ineffective national leader. We are already the laughing-stock of the world, because of the inane policies and naked self-interest borne by President Trump's greed and corruption; he considers no American principle too sacrosanct to ignore. Breaking treaties right and left, dalliances with dictators and murderers, allowing the highest bidders to get whatever they want: These are all examples of the corrupted Trump administration and the Senate that continues to give cover and protection from any legislative oversight.

I will do everything I can to be a voice and to vote for change, but it is up to ALL of us. I pray that we do wake up and create a more balanced approach between individual rights and societal rights. Right now, the judiciary will be infected by ideologues who do not believe in the average person. Instead, they believe in White male privilege and money. We have already seen Chief Justice Roberts complicit in keeping Trump in power as Trump tries to suppress the vote. This does not bode well for free and fair elections.

— May 2020

Bio

Having grown up in Texas 1967-1985, Hyun was shocked by the 2020 rise in hate crimes against Asian Americans, particularly by the Sam's Club incident in Midland, Texas. Not one to wring her hands, she activated her network of friends and friends of friends to form the Asian American Anthology. This has been just over an historic year of elections, insurrections and hate crime incidents. These are just a snapshot of things as they were happening and our responses to them on Facebook.

"I Survived Childhood: A Memoir of Abandonment, Betrayal and Healing" is the story of Hyun Martin's journey from post-war South Korea to a trailer park in Texas, to the nation's capital. Her story is about a Korean immigrant, adopted by the family of a white American serviceman, who went on to grow up with aThis Asianbuse and incest in an alcoholic biracial household.

Martin was adopted at the age of three and reunited with her birth parents as a teenager. She struggled to find her identity as a Korean immigrant, as an adoptee, and as an American in a family structure that consisted of constant stress and fear of further betrayal and abandonment. She built a life for herself after high school but did not reconcile the abuse she suffered until she became a woman in her '50's. Writing this book, working with support groups, and networking with fellow survivors she emerged with a mission: To try to end the culture of silence that allows incest and other abuse to continue.

Healer to Fortune 500 CEO's, royalty, celebrities and artists, Hyun taught and traveled around the world teaching energy medicine and massage techniques. Hyun facilitates transformational workshops on healing the inner child work in Embrace Your Child Workshop, Becoming the Author of Your Story Workshop and Shift Your Life

Workshop.

Today, Hyun Martin is a successful businesswoman, child advocate, wife, and mother of two young men. She wants to tell her story to fellow survivors and their loved ones, in order to help all those who struggle to find their way. She volunteers with Montgomery County NAMI and National NAMI Conferences in Washington, DC. She has been part of the peer recovery movement at On Our Own of Montgomery County and Maryland. She volunteers at the Light of Truth Center in Baltimore, MD as a Volunteer Coordinator.

If you would like to receive further information, a copy of the book, or to interview Hyun Martin please reach her at hyun@hyunmartin.com.

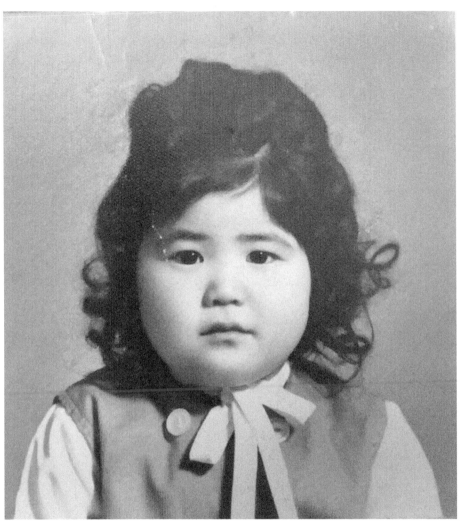

Hyun Martin Passport Photo

Hyun Martin

Mark Hagland

Yes, I Am an American—No Need to Hyphenate

As an Asian-American, I have had the same experience as my fellow Asian-Americans—the experience of being "asterisked" across my entire lifetime. That is to say, as someone who is Asian, I am never understood to be American in the sense that white people are understood to be American. I am always hyphenated, asterisked, qualified. I am not a "regular" American.

I have always known this, from the time I was a tiny child. Growing up in white America, I was teased, taunted, and socially marginalized. It was made plain to me every day that I was not like a "normal, regular" American—I was a foreigner. And so I have had the classic experience of growing up as the "perpetual foreigner." My twin brother and I ended up hyper-developing our verbal skills in English, as we were constantly told how well we spoke English—even though it was our first language.

And I ended up becoming intensively involved both in the English language, as an English major during my undergraduate college career, and then as a professional journalist for nearly 40 years now, after graduating from a top journalism school with my master's in journalism.

So, being different, being "other," being set apart, influenced my life in many ways, not only hyper-developing my verbal and written language skills, but also motivating my interest in the world—to find out how other people lived, to try to get a sense of how unusual I really was, or wasn't. And ultimately, it led me to travel to numerous foreign countries, and to learn several languages—partly out of the curiosity that

I grew up with, having grown up being marked profoundly "different." And that is good.

And then there was the added layer of being an Asian adoptee (I was born in South Korea), because most of us transracial, international adoptees experience the further marginalization of growing up with white parents, in white culture, which further marginalizes us.

And so we end up being "outside-insiders," or "inside-outsiders," both to the culture in which we grew up, and relative to the society into which we were born, but left.

I certainly had that experience when I visited South Korea three times as an adult, in 2002, 2006, and 2008, after having left as an eight-month-old infant—being a total foreigner and yet still, not a total foreigner.

In any case, in my own life, I long ago came to the realization that I would have to build my own self-confidence around my identity as an Asian-American, and as an American, because no one would simply "give" that confidence to me. And so I have. But inevitably, the only way in which I was able to build a strong self-identity as an American was to build an international identity, one built on the "citizen of the world" concept, in which I saw expansively enough my identity in a far broader context—precisely because many of the people I grew up with would never allow me to be fully normalized. And to many white Americans, I never will be.

But now, in middle age, I've finally come to a place of centering and calm regarding all of this. There are many white Americans who will never fully accept me as American, even if I've lived as an American longer than they've been alive. That is their issue, not mine. And my identity is something solidly grounded within me, and yes, I draw on the strength of some very archetypally "American" characteristics, such as self-confidence, optimism, individualism, and resilience, in having created and sustained an identity that for some others may always remain asterisked, qualified, hyphenated. If my identity is an issue, it is their issue. I am an American. And a citizen of the world. But, yes, an American. No need to hyphenate.

Day After Elections

I sincerely hope that all my white friends will reflect on and understand the great burden of sorrow that all of us who are people of color in this country (the United States) are bearing today. Contemplating the fact that something like half of the white people (and in some communities and regions, the broad majority) in this country voted for the most openly racist, xenophobic, bigoted, and bigotry-pandering president in U.S. history, is something that many of us are finding simply too much to bear. It is a deep, world-weary sorrow that we're feeling--not new, but causing acute pain in this moment, nevertheless.

Think about everything that's happened in the past four years, with a sitting president who has been spewing racism, xenophobia, and bigotry of all kinds, every single day, as well as acting out that bigotry in his official actions. I fully realize that many white people will never understand how painful it is to us POC that they have chosen to vote to reelect that monster. And yes, it is different from four years ago, because he has enacted his bigotry and his pandering to and fomenting of, bigotry, as the sitting president, not simply as a presidential candidate. He has used the power invested in his office to deliberately cause harm to people of color, immigrants, LGBTQ people, non-Christians, and all oppressed and marginalized groups in this country.

One of the fascinating--in a truly terrible way--elements of racism is how individual white people can consistently support racism across their entire lives and yet, with total ease, insist on their personal non-racism. But we people of color aren't fooled. We can see racism in words, attitudes, and actions. And this mass of votes for someone who is openly racist and whose entire presidency has been based on racism, xenophobia, bigotry of all kinds, and the othering and oppression of POC and other oppressed and marginalized Americans, speaks volumes. It virtually screams its truth.

I have gotten entangled in threads on the pages of Facebook friends whose friends have shouted their support of Donald Trump, and whose friends have absolutely rejected any insinuation or accusation that they could be racist. In this country and culture--in white culture in particular--white people imagine that racism is akin to some form of identity, such as being left-handed or Bulgarian, or something; it's not. We POC judge people based on their words, attitudes, and actions; we see what people are by what they say and what they do; it is an incredibly slippery slope to "judge hearts," as defensive white people will say; and so we don't do that. But we see people, as they reveal themselves to us. And in this moment, we're seeing who the racist white people are in this country based on their actions. A vote to reelect Donald Trump was a vote to enshrine systemic racism and to further it, in our country. PERIOD. Please don't insult us by claiming that you were just thinking about the stock market (and don't even get me started on the whole "stock market" argument, anyway). We know.

So--if there are any individuals who are friends of mine on Facebook, who still do not understand, I would implore them to search their souls to try to understand. Because this is important. And no, I will not excuse people. This is 2020, and any American who can vote can read and can learn. And no, fundamentally, this is not political; it's personal.

So yes, this is my "J'accuse." (Look it up.) And why I will not allow anyone who voted for that monster to attempt personal friendship with me. And it's up to every individual who reads this, to reflect on it and to try to understand it, if they don't. And if they don't, fine; but I will not compromise my moral compass. I will not bow. I will see and act with moral clarity. Always.

Blessings to all of my fellow POC, and to all of our white allies. The fight must go on.

A Brief Note: This Moment in America

Honestly, for many of us Asian-Americans, this week has been shattering--not just because of the savage murders of 8 people in Atlanta, 6 of them Asian-American women--but also because of the callous and in some cases, truly horrific reactions on the part of some whyt individuals in this country, who have actually mocked our tragedy (viz., Rep. Chip Roy to Rep. Grace Meng at Wednesday's House hearing on anti-Asian violence), and have attempted to dismiss and deflect--as they've done with every attack on people of color. At least this horrific mass murder has forced the mainstream news media to begin (at least for the moment) to cover in a serious way the exploding rate of hate-based attacks and aggressions on Asians/AAPIs, a crisis that has long been under-reported and under-covered.

Meanwhile, I'd like to ask my whyt friends to consider that experiencing this trauma, even through the media (meaning, not directly as someone involved in the incidents), can be profoundly destabilizing. Many of us are checking in regularly with one another this week--and I also very much appreciate that I've had a number of whyt friends reach out to me via PM on Facebook--I so appreciate you. The reality is that this situation, for so many Asian-Americans this week, has been a total emotional rollercoaster, and many are having wildly oscillating emotions from one moment to the next. There's no "right" or "wrong" way to respond emotionally to something like this. This was a form of terrorism against Asian-Americans, and there's simply no "correct" way to respond to it. But the reality is that many are in shock, and many are rightly fearful, especially of the near future. Who's to say that there won't be copycats?

The other thing that I keep trying to emphasize is how binary and simplistic the thinking around this has been among some people (yes, some whyt people). The truth is that this killing spree was racist AND it was misogynistic AND it was related to sexuality/dominance AND it involved profound mental illness AND it involved access to guns/the gun culture AND it was strongly related to right-wing evangelical culture (per sexuality) AND it related to xenophobia against recent immigrants AND it was premeditated AND it was completely deranged. I'm sick to death of the people (including some in positions of authority, i.e., police department spokespeople) who are insisting on seeing this killing spree as "one thing." It was/is many things at once, as so many terrible crimes are. Come on now--really.

Meanwhile, this week's horror reinforced two things that I've been seeing for a very long time, but which have been intensifying of late. First is the explosion in anti-Asian violence of all kinds. The mainstream media have been slow to report on it, but Asian-Americans are being assaulted in every way in this country (the US) right now: being verbally assaulted, being spat on, being punched, kicked, and shoved to the ground, and worse. Is it any surprise? Donald Trump has spent a full year--including even now, two months after being kicked out of office--intensifying his hate-filled attacks on Asian-Americans, intensifying his use of the violence-promoting terms "China virus" and "kung flu," constantly linking every negative thing involving the government of mainland China with Asian-Americans in the United States, without regard to their actual ethnicity, and in active denial of their American-ness (whether as citizens or long-term residents), and the Republicans in Congress and the statehouses, and above all, the talking heads on Fox News and across the right-wing media swamp, have been amplifying the hate-filled rhetoric. I've been agreeing with Asian-American friends that we've actually been surprised that the violence hasn't been even worse. Really.

And the second thing that's been ever-present for me this week has been this: the clarity in my mind about the overall direction of this country (the US), in which the majority of Americans are becoming increasingly progressive, accepting, and tolerant, but in which a significant minority of whyt people are becoming dramatically more intolerant and openly hate-filled than ever before. Yes, the racism was already there, but Donald Trump spent four years pouring gasoline on the flames of hatred and intolerance, and the open expression of clear racism and whyt supremacy in spaces where previously it would at least have been moderated to some extent by past sociopolitical norms, has now smashed all boundaries of control. It's like a raging wildfire now, with the right-wing racist Trump supporters/Fox News viewers/etc. shifting into a very open kind of whyt supremacy that honestly is breathtaking. Again, we POC always knew the racism was there; that's not in question. But it's becoming open season now on all people of color in this country, and it's very frightening. Of course, the percentage of whyt people who are intensifying their racism and bigotry of all kinds is below the majority; we can debate what percentage, but it tracks closely with the core Trump supporters, who now represent about maybe 20 percent of all voters and maybe 30 percent of all whyt adults (we could debate those estimates endlessly). In any case, it's not a majority of whyt people, but it's a significant plurality. And they are getting worse now--I can feel it.

They're getting worse because they're feeling threatened. They want 1950 back. Or maybe even 1850. In any case, the old boundaries are all gone now, and in the Republican Party, which is teetering towards semi-collapse, the desperation is palpable. Thus, every night on Fox News is approaching a Klan rally level of rhetoric and incitement now.

And we are rapidly becoming two societies now--two totally irreconcilable societies. The broader American society is becoming more accepting, more tolerant, more inclusive, while the right-wing racist part of our society is intensifying in its whyt supremacist ossification. I can see it incredibly clearly, and I know that many others can, too.

The bottom line really is astonishingly simple: in this ongoing sociopolitical civil war, whyt people have two choices: either to become true allies of people of color, or to support the other side. The third choice, passivity/silence, means de facto support of the racists--it really does. And we POC can see the choices that individual whyt people are making-- we really can.

Ultimately, I think that this week will have been important in having made things very clear. And, speaking for myself only, I really do see this as a profound choice for our country between good and evil. There's no nuance any longer. And we POC see that very clearly.

Thank you for reading and considering this.

Boulder, CO Shooting

Yet another blood-stained chapter in the ongoing horror of mass gun violence in this country. And beyond the horrific reality of at least ten innocent people dead, others injured, others psychologically scarred, we're about to go through the same god-awful routine again: the news media asking what the killer's motive was--as though there is a rational motivation for going into a grocery store and gunning down a whole bunch of people; the same stale debate over gun violence; the same right-wing whyt public officials saying that nothing can ever be done. WHEN WILL THIS ALL BE OVER?????

Let's just be truthful and plain-spoken about this: 1. It doesn't matter what the killer's supposed motivation was; there is literally nothing that could possibly justify or even rationally explain someone going into a grocery store and opening fire on shoppers. 2. As the news was breaking, I saw an interview with a former police chief, who noted that there were 600 mass gun events last year, and have been 100 already this year, in this country; and we're not even through March yet (OMG). 3. We have simply got to deal with the culture of toxic masculinity and the gun culture in this country, which together guarantee that these horrific mass gun murders will keep happening. 4. Per that, every single one of us living in the United States is a potential victim at any moment. The idea that this kind of despicable and shocking event couldn't happen to any one of us is a pure delusion. 5. Yes, I am going to reference the Senate filibuster. There is an actual chance, if Kyrsten Sinema and Joe Manchin can actually be persuaded to kill the filibuster, that we can get at least a bit of decent gun control legislation passed. A chance.

Who will stand up to this? Who???

— *3/22/21 Facebook post*

4/2/21 - Georgia and Gun Rights

OMG. You've just got to read this excellent report by the AP's Jeff Amy. REALLY. The Georgia Republicans were determined to EXPAND gun ownership laws, but clutched at the last moment because of fear that voters might perceive that legislation negatively--just a couple of weeks after a horrific, racist mass murder in Atlanta, and following TWO MORE mass murders in the U.S. since then. I mean, on a certain level, it's almost difficult to even know what to say...

But here's the thing: the Georgia Republicans, like the Republicans in the vast majority of states, are determined to rule through neofascism; they no longer even care who sees what they're doing. And yes, I've said it many times, and I'm going to keep saying it, every single day if need be: we're in the middle of an intense and intensifying political civil war in this country right now, and there is literally no middle ground of any kind. You're either for whyt supremacist, theocratic, ignorant, fascistic dictatorship (aka, Republicanism), or you're for the preservation of our democracy and progress on all fronts (the Democrats). There are only two sides, there's no gray area or nuance of any kind, and you can only pick one side. THAT'S IT. And if you choose to be "neutral," you're supporting the racist neofascists. It's as simple as that.

And Georgia politics is ground zero in the struggle. We absolutely MUST get the Rev. Raphael Warnock reelected next November, and also help Stacey Abrams to win the governorship, which Brian Kemp cheated her out of, four years ago. And we must go into scorched-earth battle with the Republicans in Congress and in every single state legislature in the country. PERIOD.

And yes, I'm going to keep repeating the same points over and over and over again, until everyone understands them. YOU'RE WELCOME.

Bio

Mark Hagland was born in South Korea in 1960 and adopted by white Americans. He grew up in Milwaukee, Wisconsin, but escaped. He is a professional journalist, and lives in Chicago.

Mark Hagland

Mina Chow, AIA (Asian in America)

"Face of a Nation"

Expo 2020, in Dubai, is the next World's Fair. Anyone have this on their calendar? I certainly did not. Until I spoke with Mina Chow, AIA, Senior Lecturer at the University of Southern California School of Architecture. She has spent the past 8 years eyebrow deep in the mystery that became the concept of America's presence in the World's Fair.

At one time, the Word's Fair was not only large in concept, but in presence. Attending one was a vacation destination; the United States was always looked to for innovative, forward-thinking constructs, and the idealism was at its brightest. So, what happened?

Chow's film, "Face of a Nation," explores what did indeed happen to America's presence at the highly recognized and regarded event. This 57- minute documentary depicts what she discovered and poses questions to all: the government, the American people, the architects. I watched it and was profoundly affected by the questions and why I as an American had lost touch with this behemoth event. Questions of identity began to cultivate and carve out personal space in my mind, but also where is our collective pride as a body of people—both in who we are and what we represent. Below is one of many conversations I had with Chow who faced the same quandaries.

This film was a work of passion spurring you on for nearly a decade. Tell us how it began and why.

In 2009, I was sent to China to make a short documentary for USC. I was excited to see a poster for the 2010 Shanghai World Expo. I had no idea World's Fairs were still happening, and so I was determined to film the event the following year. As a new filmmaker, I had just started learning how to direct and produce– and I wanted to make a good film. I had taken film classes in grad school, but I wasn't a confident filmmaker without the degree. I thought since I taught at a university that had excellent film and journalism schools, if I could collaborate w/ experienced faculty—the quality of the film might be better.

It didn't start as a feature film. The film began as an interdisciplinary short research film funded by 4 USC grants. Our idea was to film "the real vs. the ideal" in the design of the National Pavilions. We wanted to compare the architect's "intent" vs. the user's experience. The architect's intended ideas might be the same– or completely different from what the user's experienced. We started pre-production with this idea. But after we started filming, I realized we had stumbled on something MUCH bigger… It was a "big idea" (or theme) that would not leave me alone… for 7 years.

I doggedly pursued this "big idea" that would not let me go—and of which I would not let go. When people ask me if the film is about architecture, I tell them the film uses architecture to tell a story of the erosion of the American image as the country loses sight of its vision and values. We emphasize the role of architecture in national identity as a social issue about representation of the American people; and the importance of cultural diplomacy in our relationships to other countries.

But, trying to capture this visually and cinematically—just didn't seem enough. I sensed there was something more elusive— and also more powerful. As I kept filming, I noticed Frank Gehry, FAIA, Barton Myers, FAIA, and others alluding to an almost palpable emotion. It might be better to describe it as a "feeling." The film tries to capture a "feeling" of loss and hope.

You did not want to appear in the film, but it added a personal element I think was very successful on a few levels. What do you think?

Adding the personal element might be considered "successful" in some ways– but we also had to compromise on some ideals. When we started our film, my understanding of documentaries was they were about important social issues using traditional expert interviews to make compelling arguments. So that's how we started making "FACE OF A NATION," with expert interviews—and no personal story.

USC film school Prof. Norm Hollyn had started teaching me story and stylistic approaches. In 2010 on the plane to Shanghai, we talked about what our approach might be. I wanted to live up to certain ideals he provided: AVOID telling a story with voiceovers. AVOID putting the director in the film. At the time, I didn't know these ideals rely on excellent planning. They also rely on wisdom and patience. In other words, you really need to know what you are doing as a filmmaker. And from the beginning, I didn't know what I was doing. I STILL managed to follow these ideals for 4 years. But to finish the film with a good story, I had to abandon them.

In architecture, we start with "concepts" or ideas, and turn them into tactile, human experiences of form, space and order: to mark moments in time; and to elicit human emotion. In film, we start with ideas, creating immersive experiences using characters and story: to provoke thought; and to invoke human empathy. They are powerful when "conflict" or "opposition" is expressed in form, space and order, or in character and story. They are powerful when they engage the user's emotion or an audience's empathy. Visceral, emotional works are the most powerful.

In 2012, I felt a stab in my heart when a family member said to me, "I don't want my government to be spending my taxpayer money on a stupid building at a World's Fair." I realized then– how badly our profession justified what we did. If my own family didn't understand—

then maybe I was part of the problem. I began self-examining the intellectual "ivory tower" in which I lived, and our profession's elitism. I started learning about engaging our emotions. Over time, I made the film a love letter to my family and America. It's an appeal to all those who don't understand us– as creative people. And it's dedicated to all of America's creative people.

In 2013, I met my producer, Mitchell Block, who asked me, "Why should I watch this film?" "If I'm not an architect or designer—why should I care?" "Who got hurt?" "Who are the villains?" I answered: "You should care because you're American!" "American architects got hurt!" "The villains are complicated!" He said, "You need to answer these questions to make a good film."

By 2014, I was exhausted and willing to do ANYTHING to finish the film. We had cut together enough to sense it was actually taking shape. And I was learning a lot. I was learning slowly over time– about what makes a good story. A good story is personal with universal human themes. Personal details make stories authentic. What is personal is what Is familiar, and it's what we know. When we started the film, I had no deep understanding of story—except in the basic terms we learn as children.

I was learning about the importance of film characters—not just in fictional films, but also in documentaries. We had REAL and compelling characters like Jack Masey, Barton Myers, and Barry Howard speaking passionately– and from their heart about their experiences.

I was learning about "cinema verité," "direct cinema" or being "a fly-on-the-wall" as a documentary stylistic approach that seemed more like documenting real life authentically. Authenticity was—and still is very important to me.

I also was learning about good writing. Mitchell asked me to work with writer (Michael Rose) who asked me, "Why would you work on a film for 4 years—and not pay yourself?" I mentioned the journalists who said I'd uncovered an important, untold story. Then he asked, "How did you get interested in World's Fairs in the first place?" I blurted out, "My mom and dad got engaged at the 1964 NY World's Fair. When I was 12-yrs old, they showed me their pictures there– and that's when I wanted to become an architect."

THAT's when I started crying… It was the moment I realized that "I" was the American architect who got hurt. As the child of immigrants, I grew up hearing this was the best country in the world—and how lucky I was to be born here. I grew up patriotic with perhaps an over-inflated sense of American exceptionalism. The country that my parents came to as immigrants to start their new lives with the freedom and hope that inspired millions of immigrants—was also the country that appeared not to believe in me– as a creative, and as an American architect.

For years, filmmakers had been saying I should be in the film— because I was so passionate about the subject. I ignored what they said because already, I was the director. And I was struggling with inner demons not to "show off" or be self-promotional. It took 4 years for me to understand that what was personal to me was WHY I cared. And that I needed to make audiences FEEL and EXPERIENCE why I cared so much.

Then the REAL work began. As the director, I had to dissect which details of the character "Mina's" life served the BIGGER story—JUST AS I was going through my own catharsis. It was an emotional roller-coaster; with painful highs and lows of self-analysis. But this was not a fun ride. And it was potentially hazardous to the film's best interests. As a director, I had to be impartial; figuring out which personal details worked for the film, and cruelly cutting out huge swathes of my own story—just as I was learning about them. No director wants audiences to "roll their eyes" because the director's catharsis works its way into the film. Directors craft story for audiences to experience their own catharsis. It's a fine line.

Thankfully I had team members who were blatantly honest about which elements of my personal story might induce the "eye-roll." I was lucky to have an excellent film team willing to tell me what they thought– truthfully. It is absolutely essential to have people who are honest with you because they care about making a good film.

What sort of comments have you received since the release?

People get emotional–including my family. In Sonoma, I was stopped on the street by at least a dozen strangers who thanked me for capturing something they'd been feeling for a long time. A lot of people offered help to lobby Congress for change. Some people think Congress will never change about the issues we bring up in the film. But the only choice I have is– to hope. After all– what ELSE is there?

We sold out at the ADFF DC at the National Building Museum. We got a standing ovation at the ADFF LA. Screenings have been well-attended. I was happy to get into (3) of the Architecture and Design Film Festivals (ADFF) in New York City, Washington, D. C., Los Angeles, but when we got into the 21st Annual Sonoma International Film festival (SIFF)–one of the top 25 film festivals (rated by Movie Maker magazine)—I was so ecstatic. It meant we hadn't failed. We had succeeded in reaching beyond the design profession.

The film has caught the attention of the State Department; affecting change in their Expo bid process by clarifying U.S. law, and requiring all bids to address American architectural excellence. We are in dialog with the State Department to license the film and there are multiple offers to screen nationally and internationally.

What is next on your agenda?

We also just completed our 10th screening since world-premiering at ADFF NYC on Nov. 3, 2017. We screen in Pittsburgh this Thursday, May 24, 2018. It's turning out to be a busy year. We are arranging screenings throughout various AIA chapters, and other venues are being scheduled. Please follow our website to stay tuned for screenings in your area (www.faceofanationmovie.com).

What would you recommend people do about America's absence in the World's Fair?

Absence can be a problem. It's not good to be invisible. If you think this film has made its case, then please contact your congressperson, and ask them to support American participation at World's Fairs. Ask them to support American excellence in creativity in our participation.

Mina Chow

Ai-Ling Louie

Whose America?

I was parking my car in an Ikea parking lot one day when I heard loud, insistent honking and saw a man leaning out of his car window and screaming at me, "You B****, that's my space! Go back to China, where you belong!" I was shocked and hadn't realized someone else was trying to park in that space. Fear overcame me—I didn't know what to say.

This kind of insult keeps happening to me when I'm not expecting it. I feel tongue-tied and don't reply. Then I feel badly that I didn't defend myself and my race. There is so much that is wrong with what he said to me. Why can't I have something ready to say?

Here is the long version:

Anthropologists are finding that the first people who came to what is now the United States came from Asia. The earliest records now place humans here around 15,500 years ago. This is dated from stone tool fragments found in Buttermilk, Texas[1] and other evidence. Footprints, human bones, stone tools, and butchered animal remains, have been dated from early peoples in the Americas. At this time, the continents of Asia and North America were connected by a land bridge called Beringea, and humans probably walked across Beringea and took dugout canoes from Beringea to North America. American Indians are descendants of those Asians.

That's right—we were here first! This land was a continent fully populated by natives descended from Asians.

Here is the history of the United States of America the man from the parking lot should have learned in elementary school:

North America was populated by people whose ancestors came from Siberia in Asia. They walked across a strip of land that once connected Asia and North America, or they took their canoes and landed on the shores of what is now Washington state and the state of California. There were many groups of Native Americans, not one people. They each had their own language, government, and ways of farming and hunting. They shared a deep respect for the earth that gave them life, and the animals that gave their lives to them. The tribe or group lived on the land that they needed and then moved on.

At the end of the 1400's tall ships, unlike the Natives had ever seen before, came to their shores. On these ships, were very strange people with very light skin and hair. They spoke in languages no one understood. The Natives thought they were gods. They gave the gods gifts of food and skins to warm them. Soon, they saw they were not gods but people. The new arrivals seemed friendly at first, but they brought with them powerful weapons that killed animals and Native people with loud noises. They made wooden walls and prevented Natives from coming into these walled off areas, even though the new people freely came and went from the Native villages. They brought queer animals that ate up and trampled the Natives' corn and squash crops. Then, the Natives began dying. The new people had brought diseases with them. Diseases, like none ever seen before, sickened whole families, whole tribes, and they died in great numbers—year after year, more dying—America's first great pandemic.

That history of the clash of two great civilizations is what our children and our adults should have in their minds when the Anti-China and Anti-Asian rhetoric comes to light in our country.

So next time, someone yells, "Go back to China!" I'll know what to yell back,

"No, you go back to Europe! Asians were here first!"

History informs the present, but the present and the future don't have to follow the past. The America where I want to live is the one I see in my grandson's public school classroom: children of all colors in the same building— adults, committed to nurturing each child according to his/her needs. The public school is not without friction. The adults in the room work help the children see each other as equals, and this, in turn, helps all succeed.

1. Gannon, Megan. "When Did Humans Reach North America? The Question Keeps Getting More Complex". Discover Magazine. September 19, 2019. discoverymagazine.com

Bio

Ai-Ling Louie is the author of 5 children's books: Yeh Shen; a Cinderella Story from China, Philomel/Putnam, and biographies of Vera Wang, Yo-Yo and Yeou-Cheng Ma, Kalpana Chawla, and Patsy Mink, all published by her own press, Dragoneagle Press at dragoneagle.com. Ms. Louie lives in Maryland and is the proud grandmother of three grandchildren.

Ai-Ling by N. Solomon

Ai-Ling with Grandsons by E. R. Prange

Phil Tajitsu Nash

Mother's Day 2021

Happy Mother's Day! Given all that has been happening in the world lately, I hope we can give you breakfast in bed AND a commitment to ending an unsustainable system that gives unfair unearned privileges to men.

I am grateful to my mom, Yoneko Tajitsu Nash, who overcame confinement in the World War II Japanese American concentration camps and other obstacles to live a life of purpose. Aside from making PBJ sandwiches for whichever kids happened to be in our house at lunchtime, she also served as PTA president, read and sang to us at the local library, and provided me with an example of how to make social change on both systemic and interpersonal levels at the same time.

Mom used her nursing degree to work in the immigrant tenements of New York City's Lower East side, helping low income moms learn about well baby techniques. As a social reformer, she helped bring Blacks into the New York State Nurse's Association and supported the progressive Japanese American Committee for Democracy and Henry Agard Wallace's Progressive Party presidential candidacy in 1948 (73 years ago, they were fighting for things we are still striving for today - desegregation, a national health insurance system, an expansion of the social safety net, and nationalization of the energy safety net).

In honor of my mom, your mom and all of the mothers of the world, let's recommit ourselves to ending patriarchy and other entrenched unfairness, while spending today and every day building a world where men and women earn equal pay for comparable work, while each carrying half of the cooking, cleaning, washing and parenting load in our households.

Phil's Mom: Yoneko Tajitsu Nash

Celebrating Women's History Month

I want to give a special shout out to my Maryland State Senator, Susan C. Lee. We were part of the law student cohort that created the National Asian Pacific American Law Students Association (NAPALSA) and later the National Asian Pacific American Bar Association (NAPABA) in the 1980s. Since then, she has helped to create and sustain several Asian American and Pacific Islander (AAPI) groups both nationally and here in Maryland.

Senator Lee became a Maryland State Delegate in 2002 and State Senator in 2014, and been described as the General Assembly's leader on cyber security and innovation, identity theft, online fraud, and consumer protection issues. During her two terms as President of the Women's Caucus, she led efforts to pass legislation to fight domestic violence, sexual assault, and human trafficking; economically empower women, children and families; secure funding for statewide rape crisis centers; and authorize the placing a statue of Marylander and American hero Harriet Tubman in the United States Capitol.

While she has become an expert in a broad range of issues, Senator Lee has not forgotten her AAPI roots. For example, given the horrific killings in Atlanta this week, she was asked to give remarks on the floor of the Maryland Senate (see video and text below), and is leading efforts to make Maryland safe for AAPIs - and all of us. Thank you, Senator Lee!!

— March 2021 Facebook post

Challenging the New Culture of Silence: From a Teacher Activist

Exactly 50 years ago, as the first English edition of Brazilian educator Paulo Freire's Pedagogy of the Oppressed was being published in the United States, his friend and fellow educator-activist Richard Shaull noted that Freire's analysis applied to the U.S. as well as Brazil: "Our advanced technological society is rapidly making objects of us and subtly programming us into conformity to the logic of its system. To the degree that this happens, we are also becoming submerged in a new 'Culture of Silence.'" (Freire, Paulo, Pedagogy of the Oppressed, NY: Seabury Press, 1970, p. 14).

Looking out at Brazilian society at that time, Freire saw social relations that instilled negative self images that kept the majority of people silent in the face of unfairness and exploitation. Those who had more wealth and status were extolled as deserving of their privileges, ignoring a gamed system that reinforced the idea that those on the margins were responsible for their own fates. Even do-gooders who wanted to help were trapped in their own savior complexes, often starting with the premise that the existing system that had given the do-gooders some advantages also gave them the right to lead the silenced to a better place.

When Freire came to the CUNY School of Law in 1988, he celebrated the critical pedagogy being used to both question why things were in the legal system and also give students the skills to change that system. He reminded students and faculty alike that liberatory education must allow those who have been oppressed by a system of education, or social relations, to develop the consciousness to liberate themselves from the culture that has silenced them.

Recently in the past two months, I have been thinking a lot about Freire's critique of the "Culture of Silence" while navigating this pandemic world as a teacher, activist and person. While using Zoom to teach my "Asian American Public Policy" class at the University of Maryland and trying to hold "Exit Interviews" with my students as the semester winds down, I have concluded that there are at least five ways that this pandemic is deepening the "Culture of Silence":

Increasing passivity

Promoting shame

Exacerbating marginalization

Reinforcing a negative sense of formality

Decreasing privacy

Pedagogy of the Oppressed signed by Paulo Freire when he visited CUNY School of Law. Written in Portuguese, it says "Para Phil, com a amizade de Paulo Freire, 1988 NY." (For Phil, with the friendship of Paulo Freire, 1988 NY). The visit was organized by Phil Tajitsu Nash, who was part of a nationwide collective of liberatory educators introducing Freire's work to K-12 and college classrooms.

1. Increasing Passivity

A big problem the last few years in classroom settings has been the tendency of students to hide out from classroom discussions by reading texts on their cell phones or playing games on their laptops. I personally have a rule that no one can do these things during class, reasoning with the students that they are paying their tuition dollars to get some value from each session. And so, if I am not delivering any value, then the remedy should be to provide me some feedback or complain to the administration—not to just zone out.

Unfortunately, when teaching with Zoom, a classroom-replicating online technology, it is easy for students to play games, chat or do whatever they want during the classroom session. Some students leave their screens covered up, citing lack of a functioning webcam, or else they count on my not being able to monitor all of their screens while trying to lecture and coordinate responses via Zoom's unfamiliar tools.

While students may enjoy the chance to flirt, play poker or catch up on the news during class, my concern is not with these activities, but in the ways that the student is socialized to be passive in the face of opportunities. Paulo Freire recognized that the ubiquitous, pernicious "Banking Model of Education" has bored and pacified students their whole lives—essentially teaching them that knowledge is a social currency that teachers possess and students do not. Students need to have facts "deposited" into their heads like a bank account in order to get ahead. However, as an educator who is trying to help students develop critical reasoning skills so that they can break out of the Banking education model, I'm afraid that even my clumsy use of Zoom for teaching increases the tendency toward passivity and therefore reinforces the Culture of Silence.

2. Promoting Shame

Most of us have seen how the pandemic quickly and effectively pulled back the curtain on inequality in this society. Like the dog Toto in the movie "The Wizard of Oz," the virus has pulled back the curtain on the fake "wizard" and revealed a world of grotesque wealth and privilege disparities usually hidden by a celebrity culture that falsely tells us that each of us can be fantastically wealthy and powerful, even if we are not born to privilege and wealth.

Unfortunately, instead of making the less-wealthy and less-powerful angry at the rigged game, the Culture of Silence has only increased from the shaming that comes both from inside and outside. For example, during an Exit Interview I conducted for one Asian American student in my Asian American Public Policy class, it turned out that he could not participate in the weekly Zoom classes for several reasons. First, his immigrant parents had lost their jobs and could no longer afford to pay for high speed internet access. Second, he was living in a small apartment with several siblings who needed the one family computer to do their public school homework. Finally, his small apartment afforded no venues that looked neat and presentable on a Zoom video feed, and it would have been impossible to ask his young siblings to stay quiet if he had been called upon to speak at some point during the online class session.

When I pointed out that we could find work-arounds to these issues so that he could continue participating in class, such as calling me from his cell phone and listening in to the discussion, the student declined. The shame he felt was deep, and had been reinforced by seeing the luxurious bedrooms of some of his classmates in prior Zoom conversations. Like the television commentators who place the Oxford English Dictionary on the shelf behind themselves while pontificating on the evening news, some students had gone out of their way to accentuate the privilege in their backgrounds, and this student had decided to just opt out of the game.

3. Exacerbating Marginalization

Classrooms and meeting rooms are more than a place where one person speaks and one or many people listen. Facial clues and other body language are being monitored by everyone in a class or meeting, even if they are not involved in the current dialog. As a teacher, I am constantly scanning the room to see who understands the discussion and who needs to be brought into it. This delicate dance gets easier as one masters an inclusive pedagogy, but every class or meeting session is a new interaction—built on previous ones, but still ripe with new opportunities and possibilities.

In one of my Zoom class sessions taught to 19 students, I allowed them to answer questions for twenty minutes, and stopped to pose a process question. How many men and women had spoken in the first 20 minutes? As it turned out, only two of the first seven speakers were women. Men had dominated a full 17 of the first 20 minutes.

I used this as a teachable moment to help them reflect on the effect of Zoom and similar technologies, which places all the participants in tiny boxes that come to center stage when the person in that box speaks. While the disproportionate participation of males is also noted by researchers in offline classes, I was struck by how easy it is for an otherwise shy female student to just hide in her box and not say a word for the entire class. In this instance, I made sure to call on every student, even the shy ones who were hiding, but it took consciousness on the part of the teacher to make this happen.

4. Reinforcing a Negative Sense of Formality

Teaching is partly a way to transmit knowledge, but also a way to help students develop their own moral and intellectual compasses so that they can navigate their way in the world after graduation. Lots of "learning" takes place in informal conversation before class, after class, and during office hours.

Another positive aspect of informality is that challenging the teacher is easier. As Freire and others have noted, when students are developing their critical reasoning tools, the first person they challenge is the teacher who is promoting this critical reasoning approach. Instead of taking a challenge like "How do you know this?" personally, the liberatory educator sees these challenges as the training wheel moments on the way for a student to be able to challenge bigger authority figures, institutions and practices.

Unfortunately, the public health concept of "social distancing"—a sensible tool for stopping the spread of a deadly disease—has also ended hallway conversations, office hours, and other ways of chatting informally. The Exit Interviews with my students brought back some of that informality, but they were still somewhat formal due to the technological constraints.

For example, one student used her Exit Interview to discuss her career options. I know from discussions after class earlier in the semester that she wanted to go to law school, and has started a political career by running for office on campus. However, she is living at home now with very traditional immigrant parents who want her to follow a safer and more lucrative career path. I could see her censoring herself in her word choices during our Exit Interview, even though mom and dad were not within camera frame. I made sure to not mention her run for office on campus, and made a mental note to send a follow-up email to ask about her law school and political activism plans in a future semester.

5. Decreasing Privacy

Related to the self-censorship displayed by my activist student growing up in a more traditional immigrant household was the self-censorship raised by students who understand the Big Brother implications of internet technologies. One student in my class had to return to his parental home in Asia when the dorms were closed, and the time difference and other factors made it hard for him to attend every Zoom class.

During our informal discussions before and after class in the pre-pandemic era, this student had been very voluble and very aware of the ways that internet communications were being monitored all over the world—including his country of origin. When I communicated with this student via emails and Zoom after he had returned home to Asia, I was struck by the way his persona had been tamped down, and his more critical view of Big Brother-type policies was not verbalized.

Given the limited nature of our communications in the last few weeks of class, it is hard to say for sure whether decreased privacy, or the fear of violating societal norms, had led to the silencing of this brilliant young mind. However, the limitations of communication through Zoom and other issues elevated by the pandemic culture have raised a red flag that must be addressed if we are to continue challenging the Culture of Silence.

Coda: Challenging the New Culture of Silence

You can date a movie by noting the technologies on display: a telegraph from the pre-telephone era, a black-and-white TV from the pre-color TV era, and a phone booth from the pre-cell phone era. Some day in the future, we may look back and wonder how students were taught in the pre-Zoom era.

No matter what the future holds, it is imperative that every liberatory educator, student, and activist reflect on how the tools they are using, and the practices they are following, are either reinforcing or challenging the new Culture of Silence. For example, consider these ideas:

Challenging passivity: Can you reflect back to your students, colleagues or friends the ways that their actions are reinforcing their own passivity?

Challenging the notion of shame: Can you help a student, colleague or friend to understand that shame is an internalized way to keep them silenced?

Challenging marginalization: Can you use process questions to focus a spotlight on ways that individuals or groups are being marginalized?

Challenging the notion of fake formality: Can you figure out ways to create space for a student, colleague or friend that wants to explore career options and life options that may be beyond those being imposed on them by family or societal constraints?

Challenging incursions on privacy: Can you create ways for students, colleagues and friends to come to their own understanding of the ways that our civil rights and civil liberties are being constrained in the pandemic age?

Aside from these strategies to help others address these issues, consider how you personally are going to use your time, talents and energies to challenge the new Culture of Silence. As Paulo Friere himself said in The Politics of Education, "Washing one's hands of the conflict between the powerful and the powerless means to side with the powerful, not to be neutral." (Freire, Paulo, The Politics of Education: Culture, Power and Liberation, Westport, CTs: Greenwood Publishing Group, 1985, p. 122

NAMI Press Release

The National Alliance on Mental Illness (NAMI) released the following press release. It contains very important insights and resources regarding mental health issues now facing Asian American and Pacific Islander individuals and communities. As a teacher, I can tell you that there are many students and other people who are suffering inside. Please affirmatively reach out and, if necessary, share the resource list. Thank you.

NAMI Facebook site: https://www.facebook.com/NAMI/posts/10160157816192316 (shareable original for those who want to share)

NAMI WEBSITE: https://www.nami.org/Press-Media/Press-Releases/2021/NAMI-Statement-on-Violence-Against-Asian-American-Community

##########

FROM THE NAMI PRESS RELEASE

NAMI Statement on Violence Against Asian American Community

Mar 18 2021

ARLINGTON, VA -- The National Alliance on Mental Illness (NAMI) today released the following statement from NAMI CEO Daniel H. Gillison Jr., regarding the recent violence against members of the Asian American community.

"We are deeply saddened by this traumatic event in Atlanta that cost eight people their lives.

"NAMI condemns all acts of violence and discrimination directed toward members of the Asian American community. In the same way we fight discrimination against people with mental illness, we stand united against racist and violent acts against any particular community.

"The effects of racial trauma on mental health are profound and cannot be ignored. As the nation's largest grassroots mental health organization, it is our responsibility to serve all. We offer our resources to help members of Asian American community to seek mental health care and to heal.

Racism is a public health crisis, and we stand with the Asian American community as they go through this painful experience. NAMI is here for you and you are not alone."

RESOURCES

(NOTE - all of these are hit links at the NAMI website or Facebook page)

NAMI Family & Friends

A free 90-minute or four-hour seminar, with an e-book available in three Asian languages: Chinese, Korean and Vietnamese.

NAMI In Our Own Voice

A stigma-busting presentation providing a model that facilitates highly individualized accounts of lived experience of mental health conditions. This video features program leaders from various racial and ethnic backgrounds.

NAMI Family-to-Family

An 8-week psychoeducation program for families and friends. A Chinese translation with cultural adaptations will be available in 2021, with online classes offered by NAMI Affiliates in a limited number of states, including California and New Jersey.

NAMI Support Groups

Peer-led and offers participants an opportunity to share their experiences and gain support from other attendees. Culturally sensitive groups are offered by NAMI Affiliates in a limited number of states, including California and New Jersey.

NAMI Blog — AAPI related posts

Where voices from diverse communities are heard on various topics.

Please note: The resources included here are not endorsed by NAMI, and NAMI is not responsible for the content of or service provided by any of these resources.

Anxiety and Depression Association of America (ADAA) — Asian Americans/Pacific Islanders

ADAA is an international nonprofit organization dedicated to the prevention, treatment, and cure of anxiety, depression, OCD, PTSD, and co-occurring disorders through education, practice and research. It has a dedicated webpage on AAPI resources and research information.

Asian American Health Initiative (AAHI)

AAHI is a health and wellness initiative of Maryland's Montgomery County Department of Health and Human Services. Its website is available in four Asian languages: Traditional Chinese, Hindi, Korean and Vietnamese.

Asian American Psychological Association (AAPA)

AAPA is a San Francisco-based non-profit organization of Asian American mental health professionals, with the mission of advancing the mental health and well-being of Asian American communities through research, professional practice, education and policy.

[Note - lots more resources available at the NAMI website] https://www.nami.org/Press-Media/Press-Releases/2021/NAMI-Statement-on-Violence-Against-Asian-American-Community]

Phil Taiitsu Nash

Susan C. Lee

Remarks in the Maryland State Senate

March 17, 2021

Annapolis, Maryland: Maryland Senate President Senator Bill Ferguson and Majority Whip Senator Susan C. Lee spoke on the senate floor to denounce and call for everyone to unite and work together to strongly stand up against the surge in racially motivated attacks and violence against Asian Americans and Pacific Islanders, particularly in light of the horrific shooting and murder of eight people in Atlanta, Georgia, six being women of Asian descent."

"Senator Lee said, "We as political leaders must not only strongly denounce these terrible hate crimes, but also work with our AAPI community to shine light on this dangerous uptick, conduct public information campaigns, encourage victims or witnesses to speak up and report those crimes, work with Department of Justice, other agencies, prosecutors, and law enforcement and forge coalitions with leaders of other communities to protect and keep our families and community safe."

"Around the country, there have been chilling reports of the murder of an elderly Thai American man taking a walk and Chinese American seniors being assaulted in California; in Texas, a Burmese American father and his sons stabbed, incurring major head wounds; and an Asian American woman in NYC subway being assaulted. Even Montgomery County has not been immune from these disturbing incidents, with a Rockville Chinese American family's home being attacked twice and an Asian American woman in Bethesda threatened, but fortunately halted by intervening bystanders.

"Many point to the toxic political rhetoric, disparaging statements made against immigrants, people of color, women and people of all backgrounds by former President Trump and some in the highest offices, such as calling Covid-19 the "Kung Flu" or "China Virus", as contributing to making AAPIs the easy targets of violence and scapegoating, especially some of the most vulnerable and helpless. Throughout history, despite facing overwhelming discrimination even in the face of the Chinese Exclusion Act, AAPIs have help build America through their significant contributions in a myriad of fields and raised funds to donate hundreds of thousands of PPEs for frontline health care providers and first responders during this pandemic.

"Many have served America in the US Armed Forces, including my father who was a World War II US Navy Veteran who defended freedom on the perilous Atlanta and Pacific during one of the darkest times in the history of the world and was part of the "Greatest Generation." Often the achievements and contributions of AAPIs have been marginalized and they have been perceived as foreigners and not as Americans. Senator Lee noted, "New immigrants are now building on what has been accomplished by previous generations.

"What makes our country unique is our rich diversity and those things we all hold in common as Americans. It is important that all our communities unite and come together to fight hate, racism and injustice so that we can make this a better world for all individuals, families and future generations."

https://drive.google.com/file/d/1XE721a0LMW4pJ2OSwg-hOPFDAH7l-aBG/view

https://www.mdsenate.com/senator-susan-lee/

Bio

Senate Majority Whip
Maryland State Senate, District 16

Senator Susan C. Lee, an attorney, has served in the Maryland State Senate since 2015 and also was in the Maryland House of Delegates for 13 years. She is the Senate Majority Whip and a member of the Judicial Proceedings Committee, the Governor's Family Violence Council, Safe Harbor Youth Victims of Human Trafficking Workgroup; Co-Chair of the Maryland Cybersecurity Council's Law and Policy Subcommittee; a founder and past Chairman of the Maryland Legislative Asian American and Pacific Islander Caucus; and a past President of the Women's Legislative Caucus. Susan is the first Asian American elected to the Maryland State Senate.

Susan has been a leader in passing landmark laws to fight domestic violence, human and labor trafficking, child and senior abuse, sexual assault, hate crimes, home invasions, crimes against immigrants, gun violence, pay inequity, identity theft, cybercrimes, and online fraud and to support education, civil rights, telehealth, privacy rights, cybersecurity and bioscience. She authored and led passage of the *Maryland Equal Pay for Equal Work Act*, one of the strongest pay equity laws in the country, *Anti-Exploitation Act,* laws to fight threats of mass violence and terror against schools, places of worship and other places; the *True Freedom Act* to help human trafficking victims escape trafficking; and number of laws to protect victims of domestic violence and child predators. Susan led passage of a law to require Background Checks on the sale or transfer of long guns and shot guns by private and unlicensed dealers to prevent those banned from having those guns go around the law and commit violence crimes. That bill was vetoed by the Governor, but the veto was overridden this year by the Maryland

General Assembly. This year, she authored and led passage of bills to fight Ransomware and to help localities proactively develop cybersecurity strategies and programs to deter and fight serious cyberattacks that can paralyze and shut down our government, economy, hospitals, and critical infrastructures. Susan is the recipient of awards by Maryland Network Against Domestic Violence, Maryland Legislative Agenda for Women, Maryland Women's Law Center, Baltimore Child Abuse Center, Organization of Chinese Americans, Korean Community Service Center, Progressive Maryland, Equality Maryland, Maryland's 100 Women, and many other groups. She represents District 16, which includes Bethesda, Chevy Chase, Friendship Heights, Potomac, Rockville, Cabin John, and Glen Echo.

Senator Susan C. Lee

Henry Lee

An Oral History

This is an oral history of my family. The stories have been passed down five generations. My Great Great-Grandfather came to the United States in the 1870s from TaiShan (Hoishan) China after hearing stories from returning Chinese sojourners about an America with streams full of gold. Mining, and other opportunities working for the railroads. Their village, Haw Peung (Chengping according to google maps) was across the Taicheng River from the 4/9 Market (a farmer's market open on the 4th, 9th, 15th of every month and two other times in the latter half of the month). The market has grown into the city of Sijiuzhen.

After arriving in California, most likely San Francisco, he became a prospector, panning and digging for gold in and around the streams of California. The gold mining was dangerous and difficult work. There were many natural hazards traveling to and maintaining a gold claim in the wilderness. There were dangers of dealing with disease, disputes and violence over claims and transporting the gold. These latter dangers were often more life threatening than the ones posed by nature. The Chinese miners all knew the story of the Massacre on the Snake River in Oregon where 34 Chinese miners were killed over gold.

There were other stories of claim jumping and murder. Few if any of the white men who reportedly did the killings were ever convicted. When the easy gold was panned out, many of the Chinese gold miners began working for the Railroads because it was a guaranteed paycheck. The Railroad companies paid Chinese workers half the wages and benefits they paid to white workers. The Chinese took those jobs because it paid more than other available jobs and allowed them to maintain a community with other Chinese men. After my Great Great-Grandfather began working for the railroad, he quickly realized the dangers of a railroad laborer. He decided that he was more likely to survive as a support worker, cooking and running supplies than the men who were digging, dynamiting, and laying rail.

In the 1890s, my Great Grandfather decided that he was coming to America to help his father and to access the opportunities not available in TaiShan. The Chinese Exclusionary Act of 1883 had been passed, limiting Chinese from coming to America. The Chinese were the first "illegal immigrants" in the United States. He travelled from TaiShan to the trading ports of Guangzhou. He paid an acquaintance who was working the docks to sneak him onto the steamer ship in a sack of coal that was used to fuel the boilers supplying power to the ship.

His biggest fear was being thrown into the steamship boiler furnaces while he was asleep in the coal bag. He would let himself out of the sack in the evenings to find food and then crawl back into the coal sack during the day. The ship finally arrived in San Francisco. He could not leave the ship by the gangplanks without passing the immigration officials. Under the cover of darkness, he left the ship by jumping off the deck and swimming the last few yards to America.

The network of Chinese societies and family societies allowed him to find his Father in California. He did not work the railroads but tried his hand at gold panning. After he found that it was difficult to pan enough gold to make a living he too went to work for the railroads. My Great-Great Grandfather and my Great Grandfather worked packing wagons and running supplies to from San Francisco to the railroad camps. They became friends with the entrepreneurs in San Francisco who owned the supply wagons. They began working for the importers driving wagons of supplies to the railroad workers. By the late 1890s they had made enough money to buy their own wagon and began selling goods to the Chinese railroad workers directly. In the early 1900s, my Great-Great Grandfather had saved enough money to returned to Taishan to buy farmland and be with family. My Great Grandfather's dry goods wagons continues to follow the railroad workers from one staging area to the next. Due to his business, he was able to obtain a "merchant" visa that allowed him to stay in the United States and sponsor associates to work with the business.

My Grandfather joined my Great Grandfather in 1900 at age 13. He sailed from China to Seattle and Portland, Oregon. In Portland, he transferred to a river steam ship that took him to Umatilla, Oregon. From Umatilla, he walked 40 miles to Pendleton with only a knap sack of clothes and food. Since my Great Grandfather had a dry goods wagon my Grandfather was also able to obtain a Merchant/business visa. This second-generation father/son business imported seeds from China to sell to the workers who grew their own gardens. They sold other Chinese "comfort" foods including dried oysters, dried salted fish, dried mushrooms, and other dried foods from Guangzhou.

Pendleton, Oregon was the location of the railhead for the Northern Pacific Railroad. It was a staging area for the Chinese railroad workers. This was where my Great Grandfather and Grandfather settled in the early 1900s. They believed Pendleton was a "safe" place because there was such a large Chinese population due to the railroad camps. The Chinese workers contributed to the local economy with railroad money and by literally building the foundation of many of the buildings on Main Street. There is the Pendleton Underground Tour that shows many of the foundations and rooms built by the Chinese workers.

The stories of the hanging and murder of Chinese populations in California and Seattle, Washington were always on their minds. The

National Guard and Federal troops had to be called out to save the Chinese population in Seattle and Los Angeles. The wives of my Great Great-Grandfather, Great Grandfather, and Grandfather never made it to America because of the Exclusionary Acts. The men had to make the trip back to TaiShan to marry and start their families before coming back to America. My Father came it to the US in 1928; he was 14. He came as a paper-son of a TaiShan man in San Francisco because by then, merchant visas were more difficult to obtain.

Railroad work was beginning to come to an end in the early 1900s. My Great Grandfather saw that coming. He closed the dry good store he had in Pendleton, Oregon and sold his wagon. He formed a partnership with three other Chinese railroad workers who cooked for many of the railroad workers. Together they opened the Oregon Cafe on Main Street. It was one of the first Chinese Restaurant in Pendleton. My Great Grandfather managed the Oregon Cafe and the other 3 partners were the cooks. The restaurant was open 24 hours a day, seven days a week. The other Chinese Restaurants in town were the Golden Rule Cafe, Hong Kong Cafe, California Restaurant, Con Dung Low, Goey's, and two Noodle Parlors.

Once the railroad camps were closed, there were not many establishments that would rent rooms or houses to Chinese men. My Grandfather often told stories of travelling to visit friends and stopping in The Dalles and John Day, Oregon. They had to sleep under the wooden sidewalks because they could not rent a room in any of the hotels. Pendleton was no different. They and their employees had a difficult time finding places to live. To address this problem, they leased part of the hotel behind the restaurant and converted it to a rooming house for them and their employees. They occupied the lower floor with 8 bedrooms. The had so many employees that they added 4 more rooms in what was the lobby and bar of the former hotel. Not all the rooms were filled, and those rooms were reserved for Chinese travelers, so they had a warm bed and company when they travelled. It was much better than sleeping under a wooden sidewalk. The landlord kept the 2nd floor for the ladies of the bordellos in the town.

Pendleton at the time was a ranching, lumbering, and farming community with many "cowboys," lumberjacks, mill workers, and farm hands. The town was the "sin city" of eastern Oregon. There were bordellos and bars throughout the city as well as gambling establishments. Today, the Pendleton Underground Museum tour includes a visit to some of these bordellos and underground rooms, opium dens, and establishments supposedly frequented by Chinese railroad workers. (Many of the artifacts in the museum came from the Oregon Cafe.)

According to my Grandfather, one of the "social advancements" the Oregon Cafe instituted was the first women's restrooms in the downtown area. My Grandfather always said one of the reasons the Oregon Cafe survived even through the Great Depression was because the women would come into the restaurant just to use the restrooms. They would stay for lunch or dinner.

The Oregon Cafe was located next to City Hall and the police station. My Grandfather cultivated good relationships with the city leaders and police. He always said that they were more likely to stop angry, racist citizens from hanging, shooting, or killing Chinese men if they knew us on a personal level. One of my first jobs in grade school was my Father filling my Radio Flyer Red wagon full of Christmas gifts, usually liquor and spirits, for the police officers, city council members, judges and other "important" city and county officials.

I remember being stopped several times by police officers on the streets or in municipal and county buildings and having my "gifts" inspected. Even though I was a minor in possession of alcohol, my gifts were never confiscated. My Grandfather would tell us that in the 1920s, during Prohibition, he was approached by City leaders to open a speakeasy and gambling establishment and share the profits. My Grandfather, being an honest upstanding man, said no. Relatives often told my Grandfather, that was his worse business decision. The gambling house was later housed in the basement of a service organization next to the city bus stop and train station until it was closed by a raid in the 1960s.

My Father arrived in Pendleton, Oregon in 1928 at the age of 14. He was a "Paper Son" of a Chinese shop keeper in San Francisco whose son had returned to TaiShan. My Grandfather paid the shopkeeper for his son's papers and identity. My Father had to memorize all the particulars of the "Paper Father's" village and house. He had to remember the number of oxen, pigs, fields, houses, bedrooms, outhouses, and the family tree of his "Paper family." After he passed the immigration questions, he was allowed entry to the US.

In Oregon, the railroad work was completed because the Northern Pacific and Union Pacific had joined their two main rail lines. Many of the Chinese railroad workers moved to Canada to help finish the railroad lines in Western Canada. The Oregon Cafe was fully staffed so my Father worked in bowling alleys as a pin setter, as a laundry man, and laborer. Even after he began working at the restaurant, he kept those jobs on a part time basis for several years.

My Father returned to TaiShan in 1937 to marry my Mother. (Her village, Nam Toon, was up the river near the village of Wanggang on Google maps.) During his time in TaiShan he organized and planned resistance to the Japanese invaders and "Bandit gangs" that roamed the countryside. He returned to Pendleton in 1939. My Mother was not allowed to come to American due to the extension(s) of the Chinese Exclusion Acts.

Despite the economic success of the Oregon Cafe, the owners and employees were Chinese, they were not allowed to own any real estate in the town. They were not allowed to homestead land to own their own farms or homes. Any money they saved was sent back to China to invest in land and businesses in Guangzhou. In other parts of the country, some Chinese immigrants were allowed to own property directly or indirectly through silent partners. Two of the partners in the Oregon Café eventually opened up their own restaurants. From 1950 to 1967, there were 6 Chinese restaurants in the town of Pendleton (15,000 pop.) and every one of them was started by men who had all worked at the Oregon Cafe.

Due to the limited investment and business opportunities, my Grandfather returned to Taishan and built the "Plum Palace" across the river from 4/9 Marketplace. It was built with gun slits, hot oil boilers on the ramparts and iron doors to defend the village from the bandits that roamed the area. During raids the villagers would flee to the enclosed courtyard with their animals behind the walls. One of the luxuries of the Tower was the toilets on each floor. The occupants did not need to go out to the outhouse to relieve themselves.

During WW II the Japanese invaders used the tower for artillery practice and until recently there were places where the bullet holes and artillery damage was noticeable. The tower is an example of the watch towers built around Kaiping and TaiShan that are one of the UNESCO World Heritage sites. My Grandfather build this tower as well as commercial buildings in Taishan and Kaiping. He bought a building on Nathan Street in Hong Kong where relatives could stay on their way to and from America and to trade in Hong Kong. Finally, as all good

Chinese "peasants," he bought the farmland around the village so that everyone would always have something to eat. He would have been much better off if he could have invested in American buildings and land.

World War II began in 1941and Pendleton prospered. There were barracks that housed over 2000 airmen in the US Air Force. It was a testing site for the aircraft being built for the war effort as well as a supplier of livestock, fruits, vegetables and grains. It was one of the training sites for General Doolittle's Raiders for their bombing run over Japan after Pearl Harbor. Every draft eligible Chinese male in the town was drafted. It was due to the town's "Chinese friendly" draft board according to my Father.

Some served in Europe, but most served in the Pacific Theater including my Father. They fought in many of the major engagements of the Pacific. They all served as gallantly as they were allowed. My father was trained as a turret ball gunner on a bomber, but after he was assigned to his unit, he was delegated to be a cook. This theater "reassignment" was true for all the Chinese men drafted from Pendleton. A few were assigned to be interpreters when troops were sent to Mainland China, but most were assigned jobs behind the combat lines. The greatest unintended consequences of being an American GI was that these men were able to bring their wives and families back to the United States as "war brides." By coming back as "war brides," the Chinese GIs avoided the immigration quota allocated to Chinese immigrants.

Not only did they bring their wives, but they were able to bring their children, including female children. Because of the War brides Act, my Father was able to bring my Mother, sister (born 1938), and two "paper brothers" (cousins) back to Pendleton. My Mother was the first Chinese woman to live in Pendleton except for maybe some Chinese women who came and left with the railroad workers. My Mother came from a village up the TaiCheng River, Nam Toon.

My sister was 13 when she arrived in the United States. She had very little formal education due to WW II. My "paper brothers" were 14 and 15. They all were placed in elementary school when they entered the public education system. They completed elementary school to high school graduation within 5 years. There was no ESOL or ESL programs. My sister remembers starting in the 1st grade as a 13-year-old. It is amazing that they were able to be educated and graduate in such a short time. My "paper brothers" were all drafted right after high school, again due to the "Chinese friendly" draft board. They served in Europe during the occupation of Germany with American Armor units. I think my older sister always hoped that they would be in the same unit as Elvis Presley.

While we were attending school, the population of Pendleton was approximately 14,500. That number was down from the WW II population of 15,000 plus. Many of the Chinese men from the railroad era had moved on to larger cities with larger Chinese communities. By 1954 there were only 5 Chinese families with children in Pendleton. The school system was 98% white. Our family grew in Pendleton. Two of my cousins and another young teenager came to live with us because their mothers were not able to come to the United States. For several years we had a large extended family consisting of 4 of her children and 5 other boys.

My Grandfather was the town elder for the Chinese in the surrounding area. He tried to ensure we were "Americanized" so that our culture, clothing, and behavior did not stand out other than the color of our skin and hair. When my Mother first came to the US; he supposedly told her that she could not wear any clothing from China because it would hinder our progress and acceptance. Our standard of behavior was to toe the line because there were going to be enough barriers for us to succeed; we did not need anyone else to go out of their way to block us or harass us.

When I began kindergarten, I did not speak, understand, or read English. (1956) I remember starting kindergarten in Colfax, Washington where my Father was a cook for the Colfax Hotel and Restaurant. Colfax was a farming town of less than 7,000 people. I remember crying because I was just thrown into kindergarten by my "paper brother" Chick. I had no friends or relatives and I understood nothing that was said because we spoke only Chinese at home. I knew nothing of the decorum or expectations in a classroom. I remember after a few days the teacher just whaled on me because I kept going to the door to leave. (Corporal punishment was accepted then.) After 6 months we returned to Pendleton because my Father was needed at the Oregon Cafe.

I started kindergarten at Hawthorne Elementary school. My teacher was Mrs. Moore who was much kinder and allowed me to listen to records after class. She would set up a Viewmaster circular slide viewer with a record player to help me learn English. I learned later she loved to collect records and was supposedly a great dancer. She worked on my English skills until the rest of the elementary school was dismissed. My cousin George, who was in the first grade, would pick me up and we would walk the mile back home. George was two years older and was brought back from China as a "Paper son" by the Louie family. When he enlisted in the Army, he changed his last name his real name, Eng. George was actually my second cousin, his grandfather was my grandfather's brother.

We moved back to Colfax, Washington before my first-grade year because my Father became the manager of the Colfax Hotel and Restaurant on Main Street. Most of the cooks and kitchen staff at the hotel were Chinese. It was then that my cousins and "paper brothers" moved into the rooms at the Oregon Cafe to live while they attended school in Pendleton. In Colfax, we had an apartment across the street from the Hotel, above the hardware store. That was the summer (1957) that Uncle Wayne drove up with my cousins, Darryl and George, and I went on my first road trip to Canada.

We drove from Colfax to Herbert, Saskatchewan to visit Uncle Wayne's Father, my Grandfather's older brother. His name was Eddie Kuen. Darryl recalls the town as a one street town with nothing for miles. It was a small railroad town that had a sizable Chinese community. The only business that they could open was a laundry, restaurant and maybe hotel. The Wong Gin family had the largest restaurant and hotel in Herbert. I am assuming that this was the hotel/ restaurant my Great Uncle worked in or was a partner.

That spring, the Colfax Hotel was destroyed by a fire. I have vivid memories of the flames of the fire shooting out of the hotel windows and huge amounts of smoke billowing out the windows and roof tops. Our apartment was across the street from the inferno. We could feel the heat of the flames through our windows. The firehouse was several blocks from the hotel, but somehow the neighboring fire departments arrived first.

Later it was determined the fire was started by an arsonist who threw flammables into the basement window. The arsonist? It was one of the officers of the city fire department. According to my parents, he delayed the activation of the fire engines until the fire could not be controlled. Before the arsonist was discovered, my Father was sued by the owners of the Hotel for not taking the proper precautions to prevent a fire. The case was dropped after the arsonist was discovered trying to set his own house on fire.

Our family moved back to Pendleton after the fire to begin anew. By this time the family realized they were never going back to Taishan and all that they had invested was gone again. First with the Japanese invasion, the Communist takeover of China, and now the Hotel fire. My Father went into a depression and was treated at the Eastern Oregon Psychiatric Center in Pendleton. (This may have been the hospital Ken Kersey used for his bestselling book and later movie, "One Flew Over the Cuckoo's Nest." The main character, McMurphy, was sent to a psychiatric hospital after transferring from the Pendleton Work Farm.) Needless to say, my Father was horrified he was at the hospital and was release after several weeks of treatment.

I returned to elementary school at Hawthorne ES. The school was a little over a mile from the house we rented off Emigrant Street. When my father was released, he went back to work at the Oregon Café. Our family was finally able to buy a house off of 2nd Street and SE Frazier Street and start living the American Dream. It was a duplex with wooden siding. It was affordable because it was next to the African American bar and social club, George's, on one side and the railroad tracks and American Legion hall across the street. The Salvation Army Church was on the other side. My sister or paper brothers who were in high school would sometimes drop me off or pick me up after school. Most of the time I would walk to school. My cousin George would meet me after school and walk home with me. He went back to his room at the Oregon Cafe and I, home.

My parents knew my Father could not stay at the Oregon Cafe long, so he searched for another place of employment. There was a rundown bar on the southern side of town on the highway running through town. It was closer to the Harris Pine Mill and the Smith cannery. They bought the bar because it came with a house next door that we could use as our living quarters. It was easier for my parents to live next to the restaurant for work because it was open 7 days a week. Being patriotic, they named the restaurant the U.S. Cafe. I remember the contractor joking with my Father that the Chinese "owned" the town because they now had the Oregon Cafe, the U.S. Cafe and the Globe Cafe (owned by the Seen family); in the past there was a Pendleton Cafe that was owned by several Chinese partners. The US Cafe catered to the men who worked at the mills, lumberyards, cannery, or were lumberjacks.

This period was probably one of the best times for my parents. We had a house with enough room for everyone. The house held my parents, my two sisters, my brother and our two paper brothers who lived on the second floor. Our family had the typical teenage coming of age drama with my sister, Fong; Jerry's dating, and Chick's less than truthful adventures. Jerry and Chick were soon drafted after high school and both went off to Europe with the Army. Jerry would come home whenever he had the opportunity. I never knew if his trips back were to see us or his girlfriend. I thought he always looked dashing in his military uniform. I don't recall Chick ever coming home. Business at the US Café was good for the most part.

Occasionally, there were the anti-Chinese comments by some of the men, but my parents were good at giving the regulars added value service, (i.e., free beer). Those regulars kept the order in the restaurant. The regulars at the restaurant would often take me hunting, usually for pheasant, duck or geese. Others would ask my parents if I could play baseball or football with the youth teams they were coaching. They would pick me up and drop me off at the restaurant and my parents would always give them some food or beer as gifts for their kindness and time. My parents never learned to drive.

My time at the Hawthorne Elementary School was a challenging period of my life. Because I did not speak or read English, I was placed in the lower tracks of classes. One of my friends from the 2nd grade remembered the Native American, Black and Chinese kids often were mistreated by other kids. I remember many times when "Ching Chong Chinaman…." and other racial slurs were sung to my face walking to or from school. There were fist fights, too many to mention. I still remember many of the boys who would trip me, push me, or fight me.

My Grandfather taught me to always watch my face because the boys always tried to go for that during fights and that I should always go for the ribs because they did not protect those areas. My Father taught me to use cold meats to place on my bruised spots, mostly around the face, so they did not become as dark. Years later, many of the boys who would pick fights with me became friendly because I played sports. I was decent enough so they stopped picking on me because they knew I could hit them just as hard on the field.

From the first grade to the 5th grade, I was always placed with the teachers who were not reputed to have the "smartest" students. There were educators who thought differently regarding the potential of Chinese students. The Junior High School Principal, Helen McCune, thought the Chinese students had vast potential. She would visit the Chinese families in the town with children. She would invite many to her house for tea. There she taught them manners, how to look people in the eye, how to shake hands, and how to behave at lunch or dinner. She was often invited to our restaurant or house to have dinner. She would give the Chinese families old discarded textbooks or books she would purchase at yard sales. She was killed in an automobile accident before I began my formal schooling, so I was never directly mentored by her. My family and the children she mentored taught me many of those etiquette and social skills.

In the 5th grade I scored very high on the assessment test. After that,

I was placed in the "average" track and over time flirted with a few of the "higher" track classes. To this day, when I return for reunions with my former classmates, I have friends who were the not considered the most accomplished students and friends who were supposedly the top students. This episode shows how those around us place "self-fulfilling" expectations on each of us and how those expectations affect us in our careers and lives. Unless we have strong values, courage, mental toughness, and work ethics, we can easily fall prey to those expectations.

The next 5 years in Pendleton were full of fateful decisions and changed our lives forever. My parents cosigned some loans for my Uncles who were managing the Oregon Cafe. They ended up misappropriating the funds and "forgot" to pay their taxes. My parents ended up with both the US Cafe and the Oregon Cafe as well as several hundreds of thousands of dollars in debt. The entire family was thrown into the breech. I was no longer a young student who could hang out and visit with my classmates. I was expected to work hard every day to help the family survive. I would stop at the restaurant in the very early morning on my way to school to start the coffee, potatoes, set up the donuts for the city coffee club. I would come home as soon as school ended to help cook and do whatever was required at the restaurant. My only relief was if I was on an athletic team. I learned to play football and managed the basketball and track teams. This was the only way I avoided working in the restaurant from the time school was dismissed to bedtime. Another task that fell to me because I was the oldest child at home was becoming the legal translator for my parents. My parents did not have any formal education beyond the 8th grade; their understanding of written English was poor and they only were skilled in "restaurant English."

In 1967, they were able to pay off most of the debt. To do that, they had to sell every property they still owned in China and Hong Kong. The farmland was appropriated by the Communist Chinese Government, but they were allowed to sell the buildings for pennies on the dollar.

We moved to Washington, DC to be closer to my sister who had married someone from Washington. My father worked at the Hilton Hotels and then for some local Chinese Restaurants. By 1969, they opened the second Chinese Restaurant in Rockville, Maryland with three other partners. No commercial banks would loan them the money to finance the new restaurant. They and their partners borrowed from the family association banks and lending clubs in Chinatown.

I began high school at Western HS in Washington. It was a majority Black high school. Even though nearly 2/3s of the student body was Black, there was a good sprinkling of kids from political, military, scientific, government and international families. I was fortunate in that I could play sports and was invited to participate in many of the school activities. Between Pendleton and Western high schools, I am fortunate to have one of the most diverse groups of friends I can ever imagine.

At the end of my first semester, I was called into the counselor's office, Mrs. Riefsnyder. She asked me what I was going to do after high school. I told her, "I am going to find a job or figure out something." She glared at me and said, "You are going to college! Come back next week and let me know where you would like to go." I came back with a list of schools, all on the west coast. She told me, "Okay, that is a start. These are the schools I want you to look at." Every one of her schools were located on the east coast or midwest. She steered me to some of the most competitive schools in the Country. Year later, I asked her what she saw in me that made her spend so much effort guiding me. It was because I scored so well on tests and did so well in the classroom, especially since neither of my parents had any formal education after the 8th grade in China. My most important attribute was that I listened to her and followed her advice.

She guided me to apply for summer jobs at the NIH where I was fortunate to have worked with some of the top scientists in the world for 10 summers. I worked in Dr. John L. Sever's Lab with Dr. David Fucillo, Renee Traub, and Dr. Horta Barbosa who gave the love of studying virology and infectious diseases. Dr. Paul McLean and Burt Slotnick taught me neurobiology in their lab. Dr. Ron Dubner taught me to train monkeys and measure their learning capacity and mapped pain pathways. Dr. Paul Weinstein and Ralph Thorsen taught me how to administer a research lab and teach. Dr. Howard Saz who was a research associate of Hans Krebs taught me to "think" biochemistry. Dr. Morris Pollard and Robert A. Good taught me immunology and its applications to cancer, tumors and infectious diseases. Dr. David Webster, my best friend taught me how to integrate the knowledge I learned to real practical applications. Each of these individuals are thought of as some of the best in their field of expertise in the world. As renowned and accomplished as those men and women were, they always took the time to discuss my career, work, and future plans. These men and women guided me through college, graduate school, professional school and taught me the value of giving back to the community and mentoring those that follow. Because of them I aspire to be a good mentor, friend, and supporter to life those that choose to work with me to attain our version of the "American Dream."

Henry Lee at the Races

Henry Lee Family

Henry Lee, DDS

Henry Lee Family

Henry Lee Family

Lily Liu

Bio

Lily is the daughter of two educators originally from China. She immigrated to the U.S. as a child. Her career was spent in the field of communications and public outreach. She is fluent in speaking Mandarin Chinese and has had her translations of the essays of contemporary Chinese women writers published in journals in the U.S. and Asia.

During the pandemic, Lily Liu encouraged us by adding beauty in photographs of flowers. I shared them on the Facebook group **Asian American Anthology: I Am An American Too** (the title of this book).

"Honor Our Elders: Spring 2021" by Lily Liu

Aryani Ong

The Day I Became An Asian American

During my middle school years, I was a sitting in a summer class, with my eyes closed. The teacher was walking us through a visualization exercise. *Imagine a mother walking out of the house. What do you see?*

I opened my eyes. "A woman with brown hair in a bun, wearing an apron and holding a pan of corn muffins," I said.

"Interesting!" the teacher said. Then I realized: I was the only minority in the room.

At that time, in the early 1980's, I was growing up in the suburbs of Houston, Texas.

Like many Asian American children at the time, I didn't see many peers who looked like me. I slipped in and out of a world that resembled a Lawrence Welk show and home - a small satellite in America of a larger family clan in Indonesia. Born in the U.S., I felt grounded when I was among my relatives, as if there were always a box in the family tree waiting for me. But in the long years between visits, I forgot. I forgot that I wasn't white, until the teacher looked at me with the satisfaction of a completed social experiment. I decided not to forget again. I muddled through an existence between belonging and not belonging.

I was alone when I watched the news about the Vincent Chin murder case. Chin was mistaken as Japanese by two white men who chased him down the street; they beat him to death with a baseball bat. Far from Detroit, Michigan, I was unaware of the layoffs in the U.S. automobile industry due to increasing sales of Japanese cars. We in Houston were dealing with our own problems with the oil bust, and waiting in long lines at the gas station.

In shock, I learned that the Chin's killers served no jail time, were given three-years' probation, and fined $3,000. To add salt to the wound, the judge said, "These weren't the kind of men you send to jail... You don't make the punishment fit the crime; you make the punishment fit the criminal."

The message was so clear that even a teenager like me understood: there were two America's – one for them, and one for us where the justice system rendered different rulings.

For me, the effects were jarring. I felt the room close around me, and I began to sink into a spot in the living room where I stood. But as suddenly as my world began to fall apart, I saw Helen Zia, the lead spokesperson and community organizer during the Chin case, appear on TV.

Prior to her appearance, I had only seen Asian faces in a laundry detergent commercial where the actors peddled an "ancient Chinese secret," so I took immediate interest in the woman.

As a native English-speaking Asian woman activist, Helen Zia was a walking new paradigm to me. She was different than any Asian woman I knew, which was a small circle comprising my mother, her friends and a school music teacher. Moreover, among the older men in the talk show, she held her ground, speaking calmly, but firmly. I was enthralled. A woman who spoke up. To me, Helen Zia represented a solution, a path, and a movement.

That day, I was born an "Asian American."

While I carried the consciousness of an Asian American from that day onward, I would not know the term until years later in 1987 when I left Houston. "Asian Americans" had been coined during the 1960's civil rights movement in California, but we were still "Orientals" in the Lone Star State.

Maybe it was because in 1980, Asian Americans, the presumed messengers, numbered only 3.3 million or 1.44% of the total U.S. population. (By comparison, in 2014, they comprised 20.3 million, or 6.36% of the general population.) Or, maybe it was because we were still writing letters by hand, making copies by mimeograph and using snail mail. In any case, the memo didn't reach us.

So I went through high school, completely unaware that the Vincent Chin case had birthed a new Asian American civil rights movement around the country. But I made new Asian American friends.

At home, I couldn't speak about Vincent Chin or my burgeoning interest in activism with my parents. They had left their homeland at a time when ethnic Chinese faced peak discrimination by the government. My extended family were forced to adopt Indonesian names, carry identity cards and eschew cultural celebrations and writings. Similar to many immigrants, my parents shunned politics. On the opposite end of the risk spectrum beckoned science, particularly chemistry. Further, my father intoned, "Chemistry is the foundation of life."

Ironically, my parents sent me to University of California Berkeley. Cal has a venerable reputation among Indonesians for training the top economists who brought the country out of poverty in the 1960's. But Cal also is a cauldron of political activism. There, during the 1960's, student activist Yuji Ichioka had brought together the different ethnic groups under the mantle "Asian Americans" to achieve political empowerment.

Landing in the Bay Area, I was overwhelmed to see the numbers of Asian Americans; they also were present in "non-traditional" fields, like media. Soon, I was attending an Asian American Journalists Association conference in Los Angeles. There, Helen Zia spoke on a panel session on the newly released documentary *Who Killed Vincent Chin?*

On campus, I embarked on a 30-year-career as an activist on Asian American issues. I went on to law school. Upon graduation, I joined the early wave of Asian Americans who staffed a growing number of Asian American organizations that established national headquarters in Washington, D.C. in the late 1990's.

As a newly minted lawyer, I focused on bias crimes against Asian Americans, advocating for stronger protections in the law; tracking incidents against Asian Americans nationally, together with Asian American civil rights groups around the country; and, crisscrossing the country, speaking to audiences. I was invited to join a U.S. experts delegation to testify before the United Nations Committee for the Elimination of Racial Discrimination in Geneva and organized speaker panels for the World Conference against Racism, Racial Discrimination, Xenophobia and Related Intolerance in Durban, South Africa. Later, I also wrote among the earliest field guides on community responses to hate crimes.

Coming full circle, I brought my daughter to meet Helen Zia a few years ago at a re-enactment of the trial of the Vincent Chin case. I've been privileged to have gotten to know Helen Zia during my career. My daughter was the same age that I was when I first saw Helen Zia on TV. We marveled at the passage of time.

To commemorate the meeting, we took this photo. I am flanked by the woman who inspired me, and the daughter whose future I work with urgency to secure.

Asian Americans: We Belong
Aryani Ong (L) with daughter (M) and Helen Zia (R)

Aryani Ong by Eric Lin

Bio

Aryani Ong is a former civil rights attorney who has worked on issues concerning Asian Americans for the last 30 years. She has worked with leading national Asian American civil rights organizations, among them Asian Americans Advancing Justice-Asian American Justice Center and OCA-Asian American Advocates. The issues that she addresses range from the balance of civil rights and national security; racial discrimination, particularly hate crimes; and, diversity, inclusion and equity in policy, media and education.

Aryani advocates for civil rights safeguards for Chinese Americans several of whom are collateral damage in the government response to the rising U.S.-China conflict. She has organized and spoken at several community dialogues, several including the FBI and U.S. Attorney's offices around the country; been invited to briefings of congressional members and staff; and worked on advocacy campaigns.

Aryani serves on a parent advisory group (APASAAG) with the local school district and the Beyond the Boundaries Working Group with Impact Silver Spring. She supports the pipeline of immigrant integration to civic participation and political empowerment. Aryani serves as Senior Advisor to the United Chinese Americans. She is active in politics.

Aryani has devoted her career to the nonprofit sector in various professional roles ranging from staff, fundraising and management to consultant and coalition partner. Additionally, she has served in leadership roles with several nonprofits, among them Communities United Against Hate (CUAH), OCA-Asian American Advocates-DC chapter, and the Conflict Resolution Center of Montgomery County (CRCMC). Aryani devoted six years as board chair and member with the Montgomery Coalition for Adult English Literacy (MCAEL) to building a countywide ESOL system to advance workforce development.

Aryani is a Leadership Montgomery graduate (class 2013). In 2019, Aryani was recognized as Maryland's Top 100 Women. She has been interviewed by Science magazine, New York Times (Chinese language edition), the Washington Post, Canadian Broadcasting Corporation, Boston magazine, South China Morning Post, CSPAN, SinoVision, DingDing TV and other ethnic media.

Aryani is working on a new blog called Six Hues to elevate stories with multi-dimensional perspectives.

Tonia Bui

Contours of My Vietnamese American Identity During the COVID-19 Pandemic

In March 2020, my husband asked over lunch about cancelling our trip to Maryland's Eastern shore. When I asked him why, he said bluntly, "Because we're Asian." His words stung me. In his own way, he was saying he did not feel safe vacationing at a location that was pre-dominantly white. I responded, "Yes, I agree. Ignorant people can easily take their anger out on us for COVID-19." And we left it at that....While unspoken, we both knew that our U.S. citizenship could not protect us from any hate crime during a pandemic as Vietnamese Americans.

My husband's reason to cancel our trip is one example of how the reference to COVID-19 as a "Chinese virus" has impacted the entire Asian American and Pacific Islander American (AAPI) community. This rhetoric dangerously creates a false perception that the pandemic was intentional to hurt non-Asian Americans. As a result, AAPIs have become targets of racial hate crimes regardless of their Asian ethnic identity. National news headlines show AAPI community members who are stabbed, beaten, yelled at, and coughed at in public spaces. Asian food and restaurant businesses are vandalized. These violent actions are nothing new because hate crimes continuously happen to many other minorities. But it is no coincidence these crimes are occurring as we live in times of distress.

Rarely have I had reservations displaying my identity as an American of Vietnamese descent. Born in Los Angeles and raised in the pre-dominantly Latino suburbs of Rialto, California, I am the daughter of Vietnamese political refugees. My parents proudly passed on their

Vietnamese customs, such as placing fruit on the alter for my ancestors, greeting my elders with a cross-armed bow, and eating most meals with fish sauce. Additionally, I inherited their repeated stories of suffering under harsh communist rule and surviving the tragedies of the Vietnam War with my aunts and uncles. I can never erase the fact that I belong to a Vietnamese family who fled a communist government.

Given my family's first-hand experiences with communism, the media coverage of protesters equating sheltering in place orders as a communist act irked me. One news outlet published a photo of a protester holding a sign that said, "social distancing = communism." While I understood that the protesters felt their freedoms were revoked, this protester's sign unsurfaced the heavy pain I have carried for over three decades of my life. As I age, I will hold on to my parents' and relatives' post-traumatic stress disorder from living under and escaping the communist Vietnam regime.

To the protesters who expressed that sheltering in place is communist, and have never experienced the physical trauma of violence and witnessed destruction of human life, let me tell you THIS is what communism looks like to my family: it's witnessing from your bedroom window a cousin's home crumble into a million pieces from a bomb explosion because of civil war; it's the government evicting you, seizing your house, land, and money because you did not support the communist party; it's enduring starvation while imprisoned in re-education/labor camps for not choosing the side of the communists during the Vietnam war. These stories tied to my family's journey to America are much too painful for me to elaborate here. But they are enough to demonstrate that sheltering in place during a pandemic is nothing compared to brutal actions of the Vietnamese communist regime. So NO, social distancing IS NOT communism.

Unlike my family, the protestor may not have direct experiences with communism to make her claims. By expressing her disgust towards the U.S. government's response to the COVID-19, the protester has redefined the word communism in modern times. Even more so, the protestor's ignorant usage of the word "communism" indirectly conceals the struggles of my family and <u>many other political refugees from Southeast Asian countries</u> like Vietnam. I can only hope that in our lifetime, the current generation of Americans will never endure the physical and emotional pain associated with leaving their native country behind because of a violent transition to an undemocratic government system. My family and I are grateful to live in the U.S., which has a democratic government that prioritizes human rights.

It breaks my heart that our AAPI community is perceived as the cause of the pandemic, and it hurts even more to see anti-social distancing protesters painting a misconstrued picture of what communism looks like. I join other AAPI activists in the movement to combat crimes against Asian Americans as the whole world treads through a challenging and evolving lifestyle. I am an American. A proud Vietnamese American. And I am here to stay.

Bio

Tonia Bui is currently a commissioner for the Montgomery County Commission for Women. She is also the founder of "Politics Within Politics," a blog for Montgomery Community Media that explores the intersections between gender, race and politics. She has appeared in the *Huffington Post*, the blog *Reappropriate*, and the podcast *Model Majority*, discussing the need for more women of color to lead political campaigns. Her work has been cited in the Third Edition of <u>Campaigns on the Cutting Edge</u> and her commentary appeared in the 2014 Edition of the <u>Harvard Asian American Policy Review</u>.

Additional, Tonia leads efforts to increase the political and civic engagement of Asian Americans at the local, state and federal level as a board member of the Asian American Political Alliance and the Maryland Democratic Party Asian American and Pacific Islanders Leadership Council. In 2017-2018, she served as the treasurer for the Hoan Dang for County Council (At-Large) campaign in Montgomery County, Maryland. Tonia's political experiences also include serving former Vice Chairman of the House Democratic Caucus, Rep. Xavier Becerra (CA-34) as a Member Outreach Assistant and former Virginia State Delegate candidate Hung Nguyen as a campaign communications director (District 67). Additionally, Tonia previously worked for the former offices of U.S. Senator Barack Obama (IL-13) and California Assembly Member Fiona Ma (CA-12).

Tonia holds a Master in Public Policy from American University and a dual Bachelor of Arts degree in Mass Communications and Gender & Women's Studies from the University of California, Berkeley. She currently resides with her husband in Silver Spring, Maryland. Follow Tonia on Twitter at @PoliticsWithin.

Tonia Bui

Hoan Dang

Political Refugee to Political Candidate

I am an American of Vietnamese descent. I was among hundreds of thousands of Vietnamese political refugees who fled the Vietnam War in 1975. Because I came to Maryland at such a young age, I am part of the 1.5 generation, since my parents are considered the first generation. It was difficult to accept and define my identity as I settled in the United States, adapting to its customs and cultural norms, let alone learning a new language during my elementary school years. Because of this transition to my new country, my American identity was something that I struggled with in my youth. My parents constantly reminded me that I was "Vietnamese" and to not abandon my Vietnamese language, culture and traditions. This bothered me, because I spoke English more fluently than Vietnamese, and I understood American culture better than Vietnamese culture; but a part of me was still "Vietnamese." I was constantly conflicted about whether I was American or Vietnamese.

My perception of identity changed after having dinner at a close friend's house one summer day. At the time, I was working as an electronics engineer at the National Weather Service (NWS), a U.S. federal government agency. During our casual dinner conversation, I shared about my recent appointment as Manager of the NWS Asian American/Pacific Islander (AAPI) Diversity Council – a role that was in addition to my engineering duties. My friend's mother, who was a first-generation immigrant from England, who probably did not understand the term "AAPI," replied to me: "You're an American of Vietnamese descent," which she explained was similarly to her considering herself as an "American of English descent."

A few days later, after reflecting on the dinner conversation, I had an "ah-hah" moment. I finally understood that I was an American of Vietnamese heritage. I was so excited because I felt equally as American as others who came from Europe or other continents over a century ago, except I recently came from Asia. I was grateful for that insight from my friend's mother because I finally understood so clearly how I fitted into the diverse fabric of America.

While it was clear to me that I was an American of Vietnamese descent, I discovered that the local community did not always view me as an American when I ran for public office in Maryland. It may seem new that the current political climate and pandemic scapegoating has increased rhetoric that portrays Asian Americans and Pacific Islanders as foreigners, but the theme of being a foreigner permeated my involvement in American politics even before the COVID-19 pandemic began.

In 2018, I ran for the Montgomery County Council (At-Large). It was so meaningful because I ran among 33 candidates of various backgrounds in the Democratic primary election. The large field of candidates demonstrated why America was so great. Those with diverse backgrounds such as mine had the right and equal opportunity to run for public office.

However, throughout the campaign, I felt perceived as someone who was not mainstream in the United States when I reached out to voters. Particularly, my Vietnamese name was difficult to pronounce by many. When I became a U.S. citizen, I did not change my name on purpose because I wanted to remind myself of my heritage. On the surface, voters did not see it this way. I began to wonder if my campaign would be viewed differently if I had a name like "John Smith"? Instead of being upset at the mispronunciation of my name, my campaign made a light-hearted, humorous video to help people pronounce my name and emphasize to voters that "Dang" was my last name, which was easy to remember.

Additionally, the press made my Asian identity the center of attention, which distracted audiences from the policy issues I wanted to address on a broader scale. Unlike some of my fellow non-Asian American candidates running, print media outlets continuously covered me as an Asian American who has only advocated for the AAPI community. The press would not highlight initiatives I have worked with local non-profits such as the George B. Learning Thomas Sr. Academy and Impact Silver Spring, to advance equity agendas among disadvantaged communities in our county. In response to the few media outlets covering my campaign, I used social media and leveraged ethnic media to spread my campaign message. I used campaign strategies that were not the status quo to validate that I was an American running for office.

But it shouldn't have to be that way. The race or ethnic background of an individual should not matter when it comes to being an American. Reflecting on my campaign experiences, I realized what I looked like had nothing to do with being an American. Rather, my participation in the democratic process, one that was built upon the ideals of democracy, freedom, and equal rights for all, was truly reflective of what it meant to be an American. What else could be more American than that?

While I did not win my election, running for office reinforced the notions of my American identity. Based on my experiences, I believe being American is about one's commitment to achieving the American ideals mentioned above. However, I feel much more progress is needed to ensure that descendants of Asian/Pacific Islander countries are accepted in the mainstream of America. I am optimistic that many more candidates with backgrounds like mine will run for public office, which will help reinforce the notion that AAPIs are Americans. Politics is just one way in which members of my community may understand how they fit into the fabric of America. The need to dispel the perception of Americans of Asian/Pacific Islander descent as foreigners remains a continued conversation in the mainstream and among ethnic communities as well.

I am proud to live in the United States, a nation made up of descendants from many diverse nationalities, uniting as one people. Our commitment to carrying out all the ideals of America is what I believe is at the heart of being American, and not what someone looks like on the outside.

My name is Hoan Dang, and I am an American of Vietnamese descent.

Hoan Dang

Bio

Hoan Dang is a community organizer, activist, and public servant in Montgomery County, Maryland. In 2018, he was a candidate for the Montgomery County Council (At-Large). For over three decades, Hoan has served on more than 15 non-profit boards, commissions and community organizations including as Commissioner of the Washington Suburban Transit Commission, board member of Committee for Montgomery, George B. Thomas, Sr. Learning Academy, Impact Silver Spring, and Chair of the Association of Vietnamese Americans. Hoan served as Chair of the Maryland Democratic Party's Asian American & Pacific Islander (AAPI) Leadership Council from 2014 to 2017 and he served on the Montgomery County Democratic Central Committee from 2010 to 2014.

Additionally, Hoan was a founding board member of the Asian American Political Alliance, a non-partisan organization that focuses on efforts to increase voter engagement and civic participation among AAPIs. Hoan works as a branch chief managing budget and procurement with the U.S. Federal Government. His prior professional experience includes working as a Corporate Auditor and Regulatory Compliance Analyst for Lockheed Martin and as an Electronics Engineer for the National Weather Service.

Hoan holds a Bachelor of Engineering degree from Vanderbilt University, and dual Masters degrees in Business Administration and Operations Research from the University of Maryland. He lives in Silver Spring, MD with his wife Tonia and their dog Lily.

Brenna Okkyeong McHugh

Poverty

Poverty should not be criminalized. Cops are so busy chasing poor people that they aren't going after the rapists, child molesters, murderers, and white collar criminals that are business people, corporate people, coaches and educators, religious leaders, doctors and healthcare professionals that prey on people in the communities they work and live in because they systemically get away with crimes and murders, won't be held accountable, and they know it.

Remembering My Aboji (Father)

Without Any Memories

June 1st never had a significant meaning to me, but four years ago, all of that changed. June 1st is apparently the date of my father's death. I do not call him my birth father, my Korean father - he is just my aboji, or my father. His death became known to me via an email composed of three of four sentences that was sent by a social worker from the adoption agency that I was processed through in Saint Paul. It stated that my father in Korea had died on June 1st, 2003, and that they were sad to share the news with me. I was notified of his passing in 2015, almost twelve years after he had passed. I remember sitting and staring at my computer, looking at the email. I felt so many different emotions. Pure shock that another piece of my past fit together so neatly, more neatly than they ever have. Shock that my father, whom I can't remember at all, had died. Curiosity arose in me. How did he pass? Had he been ill? What were the circumstances surrounding his death? Anger and resentment rose within me. I had been actively searching and writing email after email to the adoption agency prior to and after 2003, the year of his death, yet no one had felt it was important enough to tell me he had died. Again, I felt like my truth had been held captive from me. My search for my family felt like it had been for nothing, yet I also felt some odd sense of relief, knowing what I believe to be true at this moment. My father was dead. If this is true, then I could put this part of my searching to rest. Of course, adoption agencies in Korea will fabricate stories about family dying so we adoptees don't continue our searches and stop bothering the social workers. Finally, an insurmountable sense of guilt filled my heart and my mind. It's a long story that I share because I know I am not alone in my feelings of trauma, pain, hurt, and confusion.

When I arrived from Korea, I had nothing except for the clothing on my back, a pink one piece. My paperwork that I believed to be true was sent to my adoptive parents prior to my arrival. For the first twenty four years of my life, I trusted in the information that was in "my" paperwork. It stated that my parents both came from big families. I trusted that I had many aunts and uncles, perhaps thirteen or fourteen in total. The paperwork stated that my birth mother and father met through friends, and that my father had been unable to hold a steady job, and had left my mother prior to my birth. The papers said they were unmarried. I believed every word in those papers because I had nothing else. Those papers were my one link to knowing my family that I could not be with.

My anger, hurt, and distrust with men began as soon as I was old enough to read. I was five years old. I had my paperwork in a box that I kept in a drawer. Every day for years, I read and reread my paperwork. I searched for hidden nuances, for any information about my parents that I may have missed. It was always the same. I felt angry because no answers to my endless questions came from the words on those six pages, yet they were precious because again, they were all I had that described what I thought was true. At five years old, I felt anger and blamed my father in Korea for abandoning my mother while she was pregnant with me. I blamed him for being the plausible reason why she could not keep me with her, and his abandonment was he sole purpose for why I had been adopted. I hated him because I didn't know the truth at this time, and didn't know how to feel or what to do. Throughout my young childhood and throughout my young adult life, men served as constant reminders that they could leave whenever they wanted to. At age ten, a man taught me that he could touch me however and whenever he wanted to, in whatever ways he wanted, and then he could leave without having to be accountable for his monstrous acts and abandonment. I was too young, too naive, and too scared to tell someone what they had done to me. Men could hit me for simple offenses, such as not understanding my math homework (I would get dragged by my hair or hit in the face when I became frustrated due to my Dyslexia), and they could hit me until the police were threatened to be called, yet never were, and then, they could be on their merry way and act like nothing had happened. Men could treat me however they wanted to, yet I didn't have the words, the maturity, or the courage to make them stop. They lied, acted, did what they wanted to do, and left, just as I had believed my father had when he left my mother while she was pregnant with me. I was expected to keep quiet, to hold their secrets, and was expected to act as if nothing ever happened. Every time something horrible happened, I blamed my father for leaving my mother because I believed that he had, and I believed that if he had stayed with us, I would still be with them, and would not be enduring everything that can come with being adopted, as well as being abused.

In 2010, I was twenty four years old. My sister by adoption had been in Korea and studying abroad. She had gone to my adoption agency while she was there, and they translated my information in my case file. Privacy laws in Korea changed after this, so it is a miracle that I have any information at all because no one can or will legally tell me anything anymore. My sister by adoption returned home, and handed me a sealed envelope. I went to a room upstairs and closed the door. My entire world turned upside down.

The file contained information. The information I read seemed to be written about a stranger, someone I did not know. I took my original adoption papers out and put them next to this new information. The stories were completely different. My mind whirled with confusion. I felt like I was not comprehending anything, yet I was completely calm. The original paperwork stated my father had left my mother prior to my birth. This new information stated, "PARENTS WERE MARRIED". This new paperwork stated, "Two older children". At twenty four years old, I learned that I had two older siblings. I learned five years later in May 2015 that not only had my father passed, but that I had an older brother and sister. Finally, the new information stated that I had been added to my family's registry in 1999. In Korea, children must be added to the family registry to be acknowledged as citizens and members of a family. Someone who is adopted are typically never added to the family registry because it is shameful to not be able to take care of your own and adoption is considered to be very shameful, too.

All of this information. I realized that like so many Korean adoptees, my story and paperwork had been fabricated. My first story I had believed in for twenty four years had all been a lie. All of these dates. 2010 - I learned that my parents had actually been married. I had older siblings. 2015 - I learned that my father had passed away in 2003. I learned I had an older sister and brother; the gender of my siblings had not been stated prior to this. 1999 - I had been added to my family registry. I did not know what this meant.

I was in shock off and on for months after learning what I now cautiously consider my truth. I learned that many adoption agencies will lie and say that parents are unmarried because it makes babies' situations look more pathetic and thus, "more adoptable". My anger surfaced. My strong dislike for being lied to springs from having had to lie for people who have hurt me and also, being lied to by those people and being lied to for my entire life by adoption agencies. I kept asking myself why they had lied to me, why they had said my parents had not been married, and was so deeply hurt that the lies had caused me to be so resentful of my father in Korea. I had blamed him for so many years. I had not been mature enough to handle my trauma of being adopted and released my pain by being angry. In hindsight, my anger was loud and then silent, and it was a way to protect myself from all of the pain. My guilt was so immense. I apologized to my father in Korea every night for months. I knew nothing was his fault, that I displaced my anger because I didn't have any control over anything even though I had to learn how to handle my own emotions and survive the abuse by myself the best as I could. I blamed him because it was easy to do. I was upset and ashamed of myself for blaming my father because I had believed that he had abandoned my mother and me. None of that had been true, as I found out as a young adult. My world had been turned upside down, but growth and understanding about myself came from all of this, too. Since this time, I have worked to forgive myself for blaming my father in Korea, and I still struggle with feeling guilty for believing the falsified paperwork. I am also working on forgiving the adoption agency for lying about my story and so many other adoptees' stories, as well. It feels impossible to do on most days, I'll be honest. It hurts me so much to this day that because of the fabricated information about my father, I grew up distrusting men and believed they would leave or do whatever they wanted to at any time.

June 1st is a day where I remember and think about my father, a man whom I don't remember. I don't remember his face, his voice, or if he loved me. I think he must have loved me enough to add me to the family registry in 1999, thirteen years after I had been born. While I don't know the circumstances or what influenced their decision to add me to the family registry so many years later, this action proves that I exist, that I was a part of their family, and evidence that they had not forgotten me. This is what I like and choose to believe until or if a different story comes to light. My hope is to learn the place where my father rests. When I return to Korea in the near future, I will visit his resting place and share with him all about my life, and will let him know that I, his youngest child, is a survivor of many hardships, lives a wonderful life, that I am so sorry for being angry with him for so long, and will tell him that I love him even though we share no memories together.

Culture and Identity Being Affirmed vs. Negated

One of my students asked me if he could write his Hmong name next to his American name on his work. I said, "Of course, that's also a part of your name!" He told me another teacher told him to just write his American name.

Thinking more about this, teachers and educators everywhere, especially those of us who work in very diverse schools and environments, need to be very aware of important cultural and language aspects that our children/students live every, single day.

I remembered my first grade teacher and the name situation. I had written "Brenna" on the paper, followed by Okkyeong, my Korean name. I had always done that. She told me, "That's just made up. Write your real name on your paper." In true Brenna/Okkyeong fashion, I fought with her and was stubborn, refusing to erase my Korean name. I told her repeatedly, "Brenna and Okkyeong are my names!" She called my mother, who responded, "Why did you assume she was lying about that being her name, or making up a name? That is her name, just like Brenna is her name. You could have asked her about it. She knows what it means, she can spell it in English." My teacher felt horrible and asked me about its meaning, how to pronounce it, and apologized profusely. I never learned to trust her after this incident. I stopped writing Okkyeong on my paper for the majority of my school career.

I tell my students to always be proud of being Hmong or Karen, and I ask the paras and my students to teach me words in their native languages that go along with the concepts and vocabulary we are learning in reading and mathematics. I tell them we are all teachers. I told my students to write their American and Hmong or Karen names on their papers every time we do an assignment or test. Finally, I told them to be proud of their names, the meanings of their names, and that their names were given especially to them because they are each unique and posses different abilities and talents. I will always do my best to be very aware of their cultures and always acknowledge them, and ask them to teach me about their cultures.

Bio

I identify as an international, transracial Korean adoptee, and Blasian, as I am Korean and black. I was adopted by an Irish American family in Minneapolis, Minnesota, and became an American citizen when I was just over two years old. I am a survivor of abuse, rape, and sexual assault. After experiencing much pain, racism, educational negligence, and stigma from teachers throughout my school experiences as a child and adolescent, being a marginalized person - a person of culture/color being diagnosed with a learning disability, not receiving special education services until I was in eleventh grade, I made a promise to become a teacher to educate, support, advocate for, and love every child that I have the privilege to learn from and work with. I vowed to use my pain and anger as fuel for compassion, understanding, empathy, and continues learning in my field of work as an educator and advocate. I know that representation in education and our classrooms matter, and I am proud to be one of the 4.3% of teachers of culture and color in Minnesota, a percentage that angers me, and inspireA me even more to put in the necessary work with our children of culture. I have been a special education teacher in urban and/or inner city and first-ring suburban schools in Minneapolis and Saint Paul for twelve years and counting. I work with children of Hmong and Karen descent, primarily first generation Americans and English learners. My work as an educator includes not only teaching academic content, learning skills, social and emotional skills, and behavioral skills. My work has always included honoring my kids aka students' cultures, ethnicities, languages, and their narratives, encouraging them to express themselves in our shared space. I strive to be the love I never received.

I write every day, primarily about my experiences, perspectives, observations, and interactions regarding experiences with my kids aka students, dismantling racism in education, creating deliberate and intentional equitable educations for people of color and/or marginalized groups, corruption in Korean adoption and the adoption industry overall, experiences with racism as an Asian American, and sharing my experiences and journey as a transracial Korean adoptee.

Brenna Kyeong McHugh

Brian Kang

Bio

Brian Kang was born in South Korea, and immigrated to the United States at the age of 5. As an immigrant turned US Citizen, he brings the perspective of a first generation Asian American that doesn't quite feel at home in his country of origin or in his new home.

This is Brian's first published work. He incorporates his experiences of racism, privilege, struggles with depression, connection with God, and love for those who suffer into his writing.

In his life, he has a passion for social justice, fighting for human dignity, has a deep love for people, and uses Artificial Intelligence for social good as an engineer at Google, He is also the CEO of OWL Adwisors, LLC., a consulting firm providing process and technology leadership to companies he believes in.

Brian currently lives in Arlington, Massachusetts with his wife Linda, their two daughters Sophie and Penny, and their two rabbits Fuzzy and Tiger. He loves fishing and nature, is an amateur songwriter and singer, loves games, and enjoys spending time having fun with his family and friends.

Brian Kang

Brian Kang

Pamela Kim

A June 2020 BLM Protest

For those who weren't at the protest yesterday you've heard the general synopsis of what went down I'm sure. I can attest that it was white people who started escalating things after the peaceful protest concluded. I saw them on top of cop cars stomping out the lights, setting fire within. The police then started spraying pepper spray. Other cars were flipped. There were drones above dropping tear gas, cop cars on bridges. Things that looked like bottles of spray paint but were tear-gas were hurled into the crowds. Cops were shooting rubber bullets. My phone was dead at that point so I couldn't record anything.

I want to share with you some specific memories of what I saw that aren't going to be reported in the news. Visceral images.

I saw a lone white cop surrounded in the street by protestors of all races shouting, "Black Lives Matter" and "Don't shoot." I'll never forget the look on the cop's face which was hard to read. He maintained composure but was pushing down something...panic, rage, fear, guilt? I'll never know. He was silent.

I saw Black people speaking their pain and anger to the cop's face knowing they were protected by all of us.

I saw Black people dancing in the street expressing their joy surrounded by a circle of safety.

When we returned a second time to the police station I was in the front row two feet away from the line of cops guarding the building.

I saw Asian protestors being loud and aggressive. Speaking up, not being invisible.

I saw a young boy inches away from the cops. They saw him. Did the cops know that he and other children were safe before they started using pepper-spray, tear-gas and rubber bullets?

I saw my daughter...confident and up high and safely distant, taking photos. We didn't arrive together and when our eyes met across the crowd I felt both relief and fear for her being there even though it was peaceful at that point.

Which leads me to this - after I met up with my daughter we got separated again. When the cops started using force I didn't know where she was and my phone was dead. In that one instant I realized I felt the tiniest bit of what Black parents or parents of Black kids feel every day...when their kids are out riding their bikes or going to the store.

I used a friend's phone to text my daughter urging her to get away or go home. I told her I was staying and was fine. Over the next however long I used two more friends' phones to relay similar messages. But I couldn't wait for a reply. We were running back and forth. We were looking out for friends. We were flagging down medics for those who were hurt.

Only at the end when I met up with my daughter again in her car did I realize how scared she'd been. She'd called a family friend who came to sit with her until she knew I was okay. That friend abandoned her cooking to come downtown.

Other things I saw.

I saw a Black man carrying a white woman in his arms to safety because she'd been shot in the head.

I saw an organizer friend puking from the pepper-spray.

I saw another organizer friend crying and having an anxiety attack and at the same time cursing over the white instigators. We walked away for a bit.

Yet another organizer friend was shot with rubber bullets. We stood there watching from afar wondering what was going on.

I felt my own lungs burning not from Covid19 but from pepper spray.

I saw a sea of white arms suspended in the air when the cops were shooting. A protective shield.

I saw young Black Muslim women running from the police violence, shrieking. I asked if they were okay. They smiled and said yes, gave me thumbs up and said, "Black Lives Matter."

I saw non-Black Muslims protesting.

I saw disabled white people in the streets. And children of various races.

I saw eyeliner smeared across people's faces from tear-gas and saw milk poured into their eyes.

I saw the eyes of the officers two feet away from me who wouldn't look us in the eyes. They didn't seem human.

I saw a Black mother addressing this line of cops being utterly respectful, showing them pics of her young sons and thanking the cops in advance for not shooting her kids should the cops ever see them. Not an ounce of emotion on the cops' faces.

I saw all this and so much more. If you are not Black and were not there, and you simply read the news or other people's posts, it's not the same.

I can say with more conviction than ever that Black Lives Matter. And that these police are out of control and have NO business policing communities they do not represent.

For white people and non-Black people of color...

Today was one of those days where I wonder if I've actually sent a particular email or just thought about it. (Okay that happens a lot but you get my drift.)

Today was a day of accountability.

Hearing from a friend who is Black that I said some things in a meeting that rubbed her the wrong way. She very kindly and generously called me up later to let me know and we had a really productive convo and she said our talk helped a lot with what she was feeling.

It was asking for too much input from a Black friend who is already exhausted. Hearing her exhaustion and frustration and not taking it personally.

It was listening to another friend who is Black question why I had promoted the problematic BLM protest at Buckland Park as it didn't match up with her view of me. And working through to understanding.

It was providing feedback for white people on how to be better allies/accomplices. Where to donate money. Which narratives to promote. Emphasizing the necessity of Black leadership for BLM events.

It was watching others struggle...awkwardly, clumsily, gracefully, predictably, painfully, necessarily, you name it.

My point is that this is messy, complicated work. It's uncomfortable, it's exhausting and it's absolutely what we need to be doing.

If you are truly for Black Lives, keep going. Keep being accountable and keep holding others accountable.

— *Pamela Kim 6/3/20*

4/3/2021 Video and Transcript

https://www.facebook.com/pamela.k.adams/videos/
10100739553416523/

Good morning. I'm Pamela Kim. I'm a Korean adoptee and a case manager and advocate working in New Americans communities. I grew up in Brighton. People think of Brighton as being such a diverse place and in some ways it is but racism and white supremacy are everywhere. As a child I was teased and bullied. Kids made fun of my eyes. They spoke made-up languages to me on the bus. Told me I ate cat. In fifth grade it got so bad that I left the school district and started to attend a private school. I don't think I ever told my white parents that a lot of the bullying was of a racial nature. I probably assumed that they wouldn't understand my experience because they were white. Transracial adoptees learn to keep a lot to ourselves.

As a result of growing up in a white family and basically in a white society, I also developed internalized racism that I'm still working through. Being Asian American is confusing - neither Black nor white - and being an Asian American adoptee adds additional layers. It's easy to feel almost white because of our proximity to whiteness. Yet when we walk outside the world doesn't know that we grew up eating Italian or German family recipes. Some of us don't know how to use chopsticks. The point is that proximity doesn't protect us. We will always be seen as foreign, as other. No matter how good our English is. Just yesterday one of my Korean adoptee friends was walking across the street. A car stopped and somebody yelled at him, "F— you, coronavirus!" They made bowing gestures. He shared with me that these sorts of incidences are nothing new. But this one impacted him differently or more. It impacted me as well. In light of the Atlanta shooting and all of the brutal attacks toward AAPI folks that have been covered by the media lately, I found myself deeply unsettled after hearing his story. I'm thankful he's alive. I know that racism exists on a continuum and when we don't take these micro-aggressions seriously and collectively stand up for each other, that is when we end up with mass shootings like Atlanta.

Yes, the Atlanta shooting was motivated by race no matter what anyone says. As an Asian womxn [inclusive term for females **and** males of the species; we all have X chromosomes!] I know that racism and sexism are closely intertwined. Racism toward Asians is often passive and unacknowledged. Especially toward Asian womxn. Our oppression is invisible as are we - unless we are being fetishized. Growing up, my father's white friends would stare at me and tell me how beautiful I was. I was 12. They would talk about who was prettier between my sisters and me. My sisters are also Korean. I meet old white men all the time who served in Vietnam or Korea. They tell me how much they loved being in Korea. They don't say they loved the womxn but it's understood as they lustfully engulf me with their eyes. They call me Kim instead of Pam. Every time. I have friends who have been asked if their private parts are as small as their eyes. Until recently, most of us have been quiet about these things. There are many reasons why we've been quiet but now some of us are finding our voices. I personally dread public speaking and it stresses me out. As an Asian womxn, I was never encouraged to be loud or expressive in public spaces. Instead I tried to blend in. I tried to survive. But I'm here because generations of silence need to be broken and our silence hasn't protected us any more than our proximity has. Lately I've become increasingly anxious and have an almost-constant pit in my stomach. I've had nightmares of being attacked. I need to speak even if it scares me.

The model minority myth falsely presents all Asian Americans as intelligent, respectful, hardworking, obedient. Those might not seem like the worst characteristics to be stereotyped as but the model minority myth is a manifestation of white supremacy. It was created by white people to make Black people look bad. To pit our communities against one another. When we as Asian Americans subscribe to the model minority myth, we are feeding into white supremacy. When we in our AAPI communities subscribe to anti-Blackness we are upholding white supremacy.

I want to speak briefly about some of what I have observed working in refugee and immigrant communities. A few years ago we at Refugees Helping Refugees ran focus groups with Nepalese clients to try to understand more deeply some of the issues they were grappling with. One thing that came up repeatedly is that they were afraid of attacks. They were afraid of being robbed or beat up on the street. It's not only the Nepalese who are targeted but individuals from Muslim communities as well. Hijabs ripped off. They're called terrorists. And yet there is also anti-Blackness in New American communities. No one is immune when it comes to absorbing white supremacy. It's complicated and sticky. But I don't believe that should keep us from talking about it.

I also want to state clearly that I do NOT believe that the solution to all of this hate and violence is more policing. We need more understanding and connection, more education, more solidarity in dismantling all forms of white supremacy. We must call out racism and hate, change policies and fight for every single person who has been dehumanized, traumatized and targeted because of the color of their skin. I truly believe that Dr. Martin Luther King Jr. was right when he said that none of us are free until all of us are free.

I want to thank Bijaya for giving me the opportunity to speak today. I want to thank our elected officials and clergy and other community members for being here as well. Thank you for standing with AAPI communities and with People of the Global Majority.

Nadia Y. Kim, PhD

Not this time, Andrew Yang

Asian Americans always get asked to overlook racism.
Not this time.

Nadia Kim is professor of sociology at Loyola Marymount University and the author of "Imperial Citizens: Koreans and Race from Seoul to LA [amazon.com]."

There's a scene toward the end of 1974's "Blazing Saddles" — Mel Brooks's race-relations farce set in the American West — when, in a moment of crisis, the black sheriff of an all-white prairie outpost wants to enlist the help of railroad workers in a last-ditch effort to stave off a cavalcade of bandits. Seeking approval for the plan, he implores his town's civic leaders that all the workers ask is for "a little plot of land they can call their own to homestead."

After a moment of reluctance, one of the town's would-be aldermen resolves the pluralistic angst, cheerfully relenting: "Alright. We'll give some land to the niggers and the chinks. But we don't want the Irish."

The satire is simultaneously cringe-inducing and hilarious, and the point is unmistakable: Along the way, every minority group has had to fight — or is still fighting — its way into the mainstream. That even Italian and Irish immigrants who had it much easier than non-whites were expected to bear and overcome denigration with a stiff upper lip. And unfair as it is, this tradition has come to be seen as a rite of passage. One that might have a silver lining. One that might offer people of color the same path to acceptance that Italians and Irish got. One that former presidential candidate Andrew Yang just asked Asian Americans to again undergo, but this time in the face of coronavirus-inspired racial hate.

Yang is asking too much.

In a Washington Post op-ed Thursday, he proposed that in the face of harassment, threats and even being spit at, it may be incumbent upon Asian Americans to "show our American-ness in ways we never have before. We need to step up, help our neighbors, donate gear, vote, wear red white and blue, volunteer, fund aid organizations, and do everything in our power to accelerate the end of this crisis. We should show without a shadow of a doubt that we are Americans who will do our part for our country in this time of need."

There's nothing wrong, of course, with helping neighbors out or wearing red, white and blue. But not only should Asian Americans never have been asked to do any of that in order to prove that we're patriots, we already *have* done that. Collectively, we've already gone through this rite of passage. On top of that, many of us have embraced the "model minority" designation — a kind of racial insurance policy that doesn't eliminate discrimination but offers the thin consolation of sometimes being number one in second class. If there's a takeaway from the coronavirus crisis and its attendant backlash, it's that no matter how many times Asian Americans sit still for this sort of hazing, we can still be denied full membership in the American story. And that we should have learned, once and for all, that model minority status is a mirage.

At the same point in history that Japanese Americans were rounded up, stripped of their homes and businesses, and locked in concentration camps, soldiers in the all-Nisei 442nd regimental combat team [defense.gov] fought and died in World War II. Much like African American soldiers of their day, who volunteered and were drafted to serve in segregated units to demonstrate, in part, that they were part of the broader American cause, the 442nd, the most decorated military regiment in US history, bled on European battlefields to beat fascism abroad and beat back discrimination at home — to somehow convince fellow Americans that they were worthy.

Long before internment, there was the unambiguously-named Chinese Exclusion Act [avalon.law.yale.edu] of 1882. Then there was the 1930 race riot [picturethis.museumca.org] by hundreds of white men who bludgeoned Filipino male laborers, murdered one, and torched their community, just for dancing with white women in California's taxi dance halls.

Years later, there was the brutal killing of Vincent Chin [freep.com]. Years after that, there was the mass shooting [nytimes.com] at the Oak Creek, Wisconsin gurdwara. The list goes on and on.

My generation fought to move, constructively, beyond hostility that ranged from the devastating 1992 unrest in Los Angeles — that leveled Koreatown — to the seemingly trivial, but actually insidious stereotyping in popular culture: everything from the sexually-undesirable yet hyper-sexed buffoon named "Long Duk Dong [youtube.com]" in "Sixteen Candles" to the fictional "Nakatomi Plaza," the "yellow peril" backdrop of foreign corporate greed in "Die Hard," named, in real life, Fox Plaza. Kristi Yamaguchi was briefly a hero, bringing home figure-skating gold. But she soon struggled to cash in on her triumph, harder, apparently, to cast as America's sweetheart, in the mold of Nancy Kerrigan or Dorothy Hamill.

Even in the recent, politically charged fight over Asian American admissions at Harvard University, Asian Americans have been disingenuously enlisted in the retrogressive cause of undoing affirmative action [chronicle.com], under the guise of a righteous campaign against anti-Asian discrimination. If there was any doubt about who ultimately benefits from that battle, consider that it was most recently invoked in a Wall Street Journal column, deplorably titled, "Harvard's China Virus [wsj.com]" to describe affirmative action. The column more appropriately should be titled, "How to whitewash coronavirus-related racism."

Somewhere along the way, the idea — caricature, really — of a "model minority" took hold, and Asian Americans got a collective pat on the head for being the striving, deferential, good-at-math, apolitical minority group, in contrast to — as their detractors would have it — grievance-addicted black and Latino minorities who refused to assimilate.

As Matthew Lee recently wrote [nbcnews.com] for NBC News's Think, "In some instances," Asian Americans "are wielded as a 'model minority' against other groups, particularly other people of color; in others, we are cast as 'perpetual foreigners' who pose a threat to stability and order." What the current wave of anti-Asian and anti-Asian American sentiment illustrates is that you can go from wearing your red, white and blue, eating apple pie and hot dogs to being shouted at in a grocery-store parking lot and finding your car spray-painted with "Fuck Asians. Corona Virus." One day you go grocery shopping as a family and then become the two-year-old victim of an attempted stabbing. One day you're an Asian American woman reporting more sexism than your Asian American male counterparts, the next day you're an Asian American woman who is also reporting three times more Corona-related hate crimes [npr.org].

Yang, who broke barriers in the 2020 Democratic primary, surely means well. As a non-white anomaly in US politics, he was pressured to appropriate the math-nerd stereotype, and to know "a lot of doctors," as a way to put voters at ease in a political atmosphere where everyone is trying to figure out the magic formula for placating disaffected, often blue-collar white Americans. But it only reinforced model minority stereotypes, cost him the votes of more liberal Asian Americans, and left him as a poor arbiter of race relations in a political time, where everyone is coming to grips with a president who race-baits as a matter of course.

Chinese-descent and Chinese-looking bodies have historically felt the pain of rageful epithets, fists, and knifings by racists who don't care whether they're conservative or liberal, because governments, corporations, and thought leaders have been the ones to stoke such hate. Today's parallel is a white nationalist, anti-affirmative action President in Trump who seems near obsessed with racializing COVID19 as "the Chinese virus," even as Asian Americans have roundly condemned it, as dogged journalists problematize it, and as anti-Asian hate crimes have spiked (Trump finally moonwalked his comments back, but that hasn't stemmed the violence against those blamed for "Kung-flu").

Trump is therefore directly responsible for prompting racists to stab us, boycott our restaurants and stores, and cancel the AirBnB accommodations that we desperately need in this pandemic? Being a "model minority" is not helping us at all right now. We certainly can't look to our nation's leader for protection, he is too busy mocking the accents of Asian world leaders. Rather, President Trump not only embodies nativist racism, but elevates it.

Yet Yang went out of his way to downplay race in his run against Trump. His answer to most issues was a purely economic analysis, anchored by his now well-known support for universal basic income. But in the face of Trump's serial, explicit racism, Yang was too eager to play the role of the accommodating good egg — a model minority. Since not all Asian Americans are the same, he's welcome to it.

It was Yang's prerogative to run for president as a conciliator. It was his prerogative to forgive comedian Shane Gillis for racial slurs directed at him personally. It's his choice, as an Asian American, to adopt a turn-the-other-cheek approach. Many of us often have no other choice. But when Asian Americans are being blamed for a public health crisis, it's not his job to ask the rest of us to genuflect. It's not his job to tell us that acting more white will give us the keys to the mainstream. Other Asian Americans know that "Chinese virus racism" is one more in a long line of proof that that mainstream door is chained shut. These are the Asian Americans who have decided that it's just as American to wear face masks, silk, and saaris and to help our kids and aging parents at home rather than neighbors who may spit on us. This is our country. **We helped make it great. And Yang should know that.**

Bio

Nadia Y. Kim is Professor of Sociology at Loyola Marymount University and the 2018-2019 Thomas Tam Visiting Professor at The City University of New York's Graduate Center. Her research focuses on transnational experiences of US race and citizenship inequalities among Korean/Asian Americans and South Koreans in the (neo)imperial context, and among Asian and Latin@ activists for Environmental (Health) Justice in Los Angeles; she also specializes in race/gender/class intersectionality, cultural globalization, and race theorizing.

Prof. Kim is author of *Imperial Citizens: Koreans and Race from Seoul to LA* (Stanford University Press, 2008), an exploration of how Koreans and Korean immigrants have navigated American (neo)imperial race inequality and ideology since World War II and by transnationally connecting both societies. In addition to garnering two American Sociological Association book awards for *Imperial Citizens*, she has won multiple best article awards, early career awards, and teaching honors.

Prof. Kim's new book, *Killing Us Softly: Immigrant Women Activists on Race, Class, Emotions & the Body* will be published by Stanford University Press in 2021. It examines how Asian and Latin@ immigrants fight nativist racism by way of a new politics of citizenship, one that prioritizes an embodied and emotive community politics.

Nadia Y. Kim, PhD

Nadia Y. Kim

Hollee A. McGinnis

I too am an American.

I bleed red, turn white with fear, and bruise blue just like you.

Surgery to remove what was
Believed to be benign,
But there hiding
Was some cancer,
An accidental find.
Told I am so lucky.
It's so early.
It won't kill you.
But it already has.
Fear you have cancer
You can't help but
Face your most imminent
Death.
Even when you know,
Death's embrace will have to wait.
It's cold Kiss forever leaves a mark
I cannot erase.
Please don't say be grateful.
You won't die.
You won't have to say
Your good-byes.
You don't have to remind me,
Who has escaped Death's embrace.
Because still I died
In that moment, the Kiss.

Flashed my Life,
Forcing me to begin my good-byes.
Although I look the same,
Some things have
Forever changed.
I carry new scars on my body.
And betrayal and loss of trust,
That this body is not holding some
Secret, unknown, lost.
More than the cancer,
It is this lingering touch of
Death's soft Kiss
That has forever rearranged
The molecules of my Being.
Every day I get, I know is a Gift.
And with every doctor's visit
And every test
Reminders, of that Kiss.
And though the intensity will abate,
The question of how to Live,
Now that I have escaped,
Has been securely pressed.
Until Death's embrace
Comes for me once again.

— *Hollee McGinnis (also-known-as Lee Hwa Yeong)*

Fires Out, but the Embers ...

Survival (avoidance and fear), moved to rage (acknowledgement and seeing the truth of what is), returns me to centeredness. I write:

Fires out.
But the embers
Still glow.
I don't know
Which way
This will go.
The fire
Has consumed
All that I had to give.
I am now left tired.
No energy.
A vague sense
of dread.
Rage is an alright emotion,
But it tires out
Too quickly.
I am left empty.
What else instead?
Eyes wide open
That things will
Continue to go this way.
Until we are
Truly able to say
to each other:
"You are my
Brothers and Sisters.
I would NEVER
Treat you this way."
You can have

Your likes and dislikes,
Your good days and bad.
But please
STOP KILLING
Because you are mad.
Instead turn that rage
Towards the hurt that you carry,
To a culture that also says
"You are not good enough for any...."
There within you is where to begin
To learn to grow love, accepting yourself,
And then each other, as family and kin.

— *Hollee A. McGinnis, March 17, 2021, in response to the mass killing by a White Man of 8 (mostly Asian) women In Atlanta*

#StopKillingPeopleOfColor

#stopkillingwomen

#StopAsianHate

#blacklivesmatter

"Hate cannot drive out hate; only love can do that." ~~ Dr. Martin Luther King

Kimchi

Such a beautiful napa cabbage I couldn't pass up!
Restoring my soul,
in this Korean body
with food from my birth.
I didn't grow up
eating this stuff
Since I was adopted,
And when I think
about it, that hurts.
I wish some times
I could tell others
That this recipe for kimchi
Is from my mother
But it's not. There is no
Legacy being passed down.
Just a recipe from
The internet I found.
My mother taught me
The family recipe for
Sauerkraut and pork,
corned beef and cabbage,
Grandma's rolled
Christmas cookies,
And cherry yum-yum dessert.
So I toil making kimchi,
And it is a labor of love,
Healing a heart of
Her losses and feeding
Those she loves.
Yet deep in these bones
memories hold there.
I make kimchi now

Hollee A. McGinnis

Holding past, present, and future.
These hands the creation of
Many lands and cultures.
@holleemcginnis, March 28, 2021
What foods comfort you?

Hollee McGinnis

Jaclyn Skalnik

I deliberated ...

… whether I would post this or not, but here it is. Tonight while I ran out to pick up our take-out dinner at one of our favorite local restaurants, I was verbally assaulted. I'm sharing this not because I want your pity, your apologies, or feel the need to show receipts to prove that this shit actually happens. I'm sharing it because it's real, it's traumatic, and many others are experiencing similar racist aggressions right now.

I was walking out of the restaurant with food bags in hand and heading toward my car which was parked about a half block away. The restaurant is on a corner with stop lights. As I was walking, I heard a man yell "hey, can I get a massage?!" followed by laughter from other men in the same vehicle. As a reaction, I turned around and looked and saw a grey pick up truck with the driver's side window down and a white man with a hat on looking directly at me (there was no one else around me). The light turned green and he drove off. My body immediately felt a cold streak run through it and my instinct told me to run to my car, get in, and lock my doors. I was scared, angry, sad, and embarrassed. As I sat in my car, my body was trembling and I felt unsafe and violated. I immediately started to cry and I couldn't catch my breath.

I am angry that he felt like he could yell that at me. I am devastated about the recent murders of innocent Asian women in Georgia and the 150% increase of hate crimes toward Asian/AAPI's in the U.S. in the past year. I am disappointed in myself that I didn't have a better reaction. In hindsight, I should've flipped him off and yelled "fuck you, you racist asshole!" But I digress, because my body fled to safety first and who knows if I would've yelled that - if he would have turned around and followed me. I should've taken a picture of his license plate. But realistically, that would've gotten me nowhere. I keep replaying this scene in my mind but I've realized that I did nothing wrong and my reaction kept me safe. I will never drive through that intersection again without being reminded of what happened tonight. I will never see a grey pick up truck again without being reminded of what happened tonight.

Please do not tell me to "be safe" because I was being safe and my being (other than my race) had nothing to do with what happened to me. We are not safe. The Asian women in Georgia were at their place of business when they were shot dead. The Asian family in Costco was shopping when they were stabbed. The Asian man in New York City was walking home when he was stabbed in the back. The Asian woman in California was going for a jog when she was attacked after being called "Kung Flu Girl." These are just a few examples of racially motivated hate crimes that are reported. What about all the ones that are not? I do not hate being Asian, in fact, I've worked my whole life to be comfortable in my own skin and love me for who I am. What I do hate is that others feel like they can treat me and people like me with such hatred, racist, xenophobic, and sexual objectification. What I do hate is that in the past four years, Americans have been given permission to act out their explicit racism against all my BIPOC brothers and sisters and it's exhausting. I am not in the right headspace to share resources or to tell you how you can help. And right now, I cannot give my emotional labor of doing anything more than share this traumatic experience with you and do my best to educate and prepare my children for this unfair and unjust world we are leaving them.

I took this vulnerable picture of myself after getting into my car. You need to see me this way. This is real and raw.

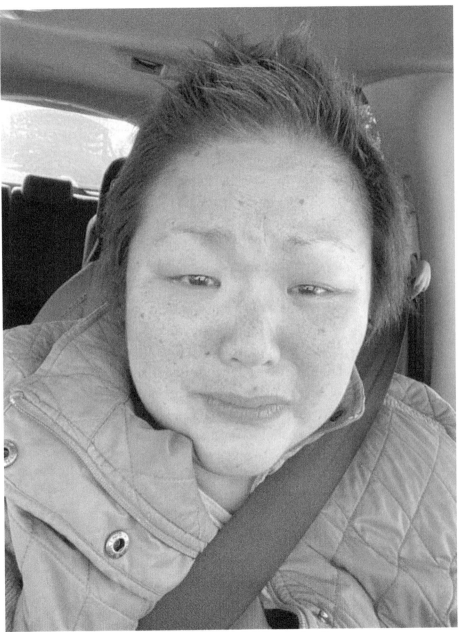

Jaclyn Skalnik (visibly shaken)

Mee Xiang

Good Intentions

Success, her name foretold,
Ah, the hope she'll hold!
My story began before birth—
The bride's worth,
her roles, what kind of
person she'll love;
When to say, and who to be,
the dread of what that meant for me.
Behold! Thy clan and elders!
Our first surviving daughter!
Fair skin, exquisite and fine,
Her beauty is yours and mine.
Perfect her as a wife,
a happily married life.
Foolish girl, away with silly dreams!
You're ready by age fourteen!-
At your age, I was this and that…
Stop eating! You'll only get fat!
Listen, so and so has a son,
he's the most desired one.
Be proper, pretty, and polite
Don't argue, don't fight.
If he beats or cheats on you,
fleeing is prison tattooed.
Twenty and no groom?
An old maid, you're doomed!
Travel, single, and solo?
She's pregnant, I just know!

Mee Xiang

Thirty! Oh, God forbids!
And still no kids?
My voice challenged theirs—
a broken record affair.
Success, my name foretold,
Ah, that trail-blazing road!

Becoming Mee

If you told the adolescent me who she'll become today, that girl—that angry, broken girl—out of politeness, would've stared right through you with a soulless smile. Pale skin. Long black hair. Withdrawn and weakened.

There may be sadness in her eyes or an utterance of nothingness. A plead to be gone. To be done. To be at peace, whatever that meant, but not always courageous enough to execute. She was playing with death. No…not quite exactly that either. She was convinced she wasn't worth living for. She believed herself to be a burden, a useless being that took up space. Death was what she deserved. It made sense. She was, simply put, just existing.

In the deepest part of her mind, she had shut off the human valve. She was numb. She was fearful and guarded, locking doors and looking over her shoulders. Paranoid. Anxious. Memories betrayed her. Voices taunted her. They whispered one night after another, chanting for her to let go, "It's so easy. You'll be free from the misery, the earthly things that have caused you greater harm than good." They enticed her and sweetened her with utopia.

Staring at glow in the dark stars left behind by the previous residents, she wandered. What were they thinking when they put them up there? No real patterns or horoscope formed. Just scattered with the purpose of pleasing loved ones. She would lie stiffly on her twin size bed, as if she was practicing to be contained by a wooden coffin, with no absolute thought of the future, no desire to dream, no hope to carry through. Who would cry for her? Who would rescue her and speak love back into her hardened heart? A Prince Charming?

Was I even allowed to have those thoughts? You know, the kind that makes you believe you can be better, that you ARE better—those aspiring thoughts.

Those ceiling high stars continued to accompany her through realms of shadows and demons. She smiled. She has taken a liking and comfort to those stars and vowed to keep them up there. She now has a place to look up to when her eyes filled with tears and sorrow or when she struggled to gasp for air. Yes, indeed, the night became a little more mesmerizing that way. They offered her light in a time of famine and drought, of eruptions and earthquakes. The world seemed beautiful in those silly instances.

I was supposed to be this and that, just like my poem, *Good Intentions*, highlighted. I was socialized to be forgiving, be giving, be modest, and be a *yes* person. Give, give, and give. So, I gave, gave, and gave some more. I qualified for a lot of the stereotypical female Asian standards: good grades, perfect attendance, a model student, cook, clean, take care of family, smart but quiet, well liked by everyone, and blah, blah, blah. I carried the weight of being *perfect* for far too long. Making a mistake almost seem unforgivable.

Quite a few people have told my present self that I wouldn't understand pain, struggle, being broke, etc., etc., because "I have it all together," that "I am always happy," or I'm "successful and going places." Honestly, I still don't know how to feel about those statements. They seem like a compliment, and yet triggering at the same time, sending me back into that place of the perfectionist trap box. It's as if my journey has been discredited, and I'm dehumanized. In reality, the process of becoming Mee has been brutal. The beginning days were full of trauma, abuse, being bullied, identity crisis, racism, body image issues, and so forth. I. Was. Just. A. Kid.

I had to learn a lot of *American things* on my own due to the language barrier and my parents being immigrants. I was a child raising my younger siblings and writing business correspondences for my parents. I missed out on after school activities and sports. I have never, I repeat, NEVER, attended a school dance. I still don't know what the birds and bees are all about. In third grade, I found out who St. Nick was and why he came days before Christmas Day. There was this whirlwind of confusion and turmoil to where I belong; I wasn't Hmong enough nor was I very American.

Eventually, during my adolescent years, I started "acting out" in my own ways, ways that were taken as being "disobedient," "rebellious," and, my favorite one, "crazy." They were a cry for help. I was trying to communicate what happened to me during my childhood years while refusing to be defined by some of the traditional ways, beliefs, gender roles, and values of the Hmong, the Christians, and the Americans.

After my adolescent years, I moved into my twenties and wanted to be in control of the things that haunted me. I learned to forgive for my own sake and allowed myself to process through the trauma, pain, and emotions. Most importantly, I sought out help outside of the Hmong community and started talking about my experiences. It was and still is a liberating and stepping stone moment for me. I was releasing all those years of silence into the world, and by doing that, I was validating what I went through.

I was bitter and full of resentment. The anger ate me alive! I hated being Hmong more than I hated being American. I even thought of legally changing my Hmong name to an American name and practiced new signatures associated with the name change. What was so great about being Hmong and American? It all seemed like a hoax, a twilight zone kind of rude awakening.

Over the years of growing up, I've come to realize I missed one important factor. I wasn't either or, and I didn't have to always choose sides. I am an Asian American, and that's what makes my experiences unique in itself. I was just well ahead of my times and paving the way for my sisters and nieces. "Trailblazing" – that's what my counselor called it.

The I in Solitude

The words alone, isolation, and loneliness have been negatively defined among many. Being single somehow ended up being a synonym of being lonely and/or selfish, which equates to something being wrong with you, or me, or him. Ah, and then *drumroll…wait for it* the questions, the judgment, the opinions, will all manifest themselves.

You're too picky, your standards are too high, do you ever want someone, how does it feel to be alone, don't you want kids, what do you do when you feel lonely, you're not getting any younger, you need to marry soon and settle down, and blah, blah, blah. Ironically, sometimes, those same people also hit me with the, "I wish I'm doing what you're doing, I should've traveled more, good on you, guys are jerk (or insert some other mean names here)," and it goes on. I've been single for 11 years, and wouldn't change a thing.

In those 11 years, I had one constant commitment, and that was to myself: to never stop growing and learning, do the things I've always wanted, define who I am and will be, and truly enjoy my own company. Simply put, no regrets. If you are in a similar position, there's nothing wrong with being single. Be with yourself first. You don't need to explain or justify anything to anyone but yourself. I started turning the stage light, that I've been shedding on others, on myself.

I planted seeds within me, watered them, nourished them with a lot of self-love, developed healthy self-care habits, learned how to survive human and natural disasters, and then simply enjoyed the fruits of my labor. I isolated myself from, or took myself out of, negative situations and people. I took time to be alone and really had to learn how to find solace in those moments. This process also required courage and honesty, of which I had to go back out and plant seeds for. And, when faced with loneliness (because I am still human after all), I sought comfort in what I already had and try not to dwell too much on finding happiness in someone else.

Through a journey of the selfs – growth, control, development, confidence, love, and care – I discovered this amazing woman. I got to know her. I talked to her. We went out on dates. We conquered the world, from cities to cities, states to states, and then crossed over to other countries. I saw her matured from a tiny seed to this beautiful tree. Her roots were grounded; they were deep. She provided shade for others without compromising who she was (something she couldn't do before). Of course, she faced many seasons, but she came out with bright colorful leaves. She laughed from the very soul and never forgot to smile. I went from this suicidal and depressed girl, full of anger, pain, bitterness, and doubts, to a woman I am proud to call my own.

When I talk about solitude, I preach on it as a journey of you getting to know yourself. Think about how many people you encounter in a day. Think about all the negative thoughts you tell yourself or hear from others. My counselor told me once, "About 80% of your thoughts are negative." EIGH-TY-PER-CENT! Because we are also creatures of habits, imagine repeating 80% of those negative thoughts to yourself, day in and day out. That's a lot of power you are letting slip away to only be destroy by negativity.

One of the first things I had to do was rewire the way I thought about others, the world, but, most importantly, myself. I went into labor and rebirth myself, feeding myself with that good stuff call positivity, of which was supposed to help me grow up to be happy and healthy. Trust me, it was no overnight miracle. Just like labor can take hours, it took a good chunk of my early to mid twenties. I'm not perfect. I do slip, make mistakes, and have my moments (almost everyday), but I knew how to get back up, which, for me, was one of the hardest obstacles to overcome. Meaning, I've also come a long way. How do you stand again after being beaten, bruised, stomped on, accused, hopeless, threatened, and so forth? How do you find a purpose when you gave up living?

I discovered this "I" in "solitude" and capitalized on it to highlight the importance of you and me as individuals. I am important. I mattered. I deserved to be happy. I can do it. Somehow, I filled up those 11 years with a lot of memories, activities, traveling, friends, and myself (of course). Live – be fully alive in the present. Meet new people, do something different, and make friends along the way. Leave. Your. Mark. Don't limit nor forget yourself in the process.

So, to end this post, I leave you with these favorite words of mine from Jeremiah 17:8 NKJV,

> For he shall be like a tree planted by the waters,
> Which spreads out its roots by the river,
> And will not fear when heat comes;
> But its leaf will be green,
> And will not be anxious in the year of drought,
> Nor will cease from yielding fruit.

Mee Xiang with Her Mom

Jenelle Anderson

Oregon

I Am Home. Yet I Don't Feel At Home

I have lived in fear or the day when Asians are persecuted. I thought it would be a war with North Korea or China, and never imagined it would be a pandemic that would bring the racists out of the woodwork. Unfortunately, that day has come and while I can have all the loving support in the world from friends and family, I no longer feel safe in the town I've lived in for most of my life. The town I call home.

The town I know every street and every restaurant, where I can give directions to any tourist, where I live and have loved for 31 years of my life. Since COVID-19 began and hearing about other incidents, I thought "that wouldn't happen here, we're in Oregon, not the deep south." Since then, I've been screamed at while walking down and street and recently as I was standing my own front yard a man screamed at me to "go the fuck home!"

Where is my home? Isn't this my home? Since I was seven years old and a year and a half since I was adopted? It's made me question the fact that some will never see me as an American. I will always be an outsider, even to well meaning folks who just want to know where I'm from. No, "where are you really from?" I don't know where I am really from.

I no longer feel accepted here and as a Korean adoptee. I would not be accepted in Korea. I am a citizen of the United States but what does that mean when someone screams at you? When you feel unsafe to walk down the street due to all the hate crimes being reported against Asian Americans? When I carry pepper spray on my belt loop for the first time in my life and always try to bring a Caucasian friend or family member with me to the store, just in case. I am not a fighter, but I will stand up for myself.

I will stand up for the fact that I am an American citizen and even though some might not think so because I was born here and I look different than everyone in this predominantly white town, this is my fate and this is my home. It saddens me that I question where I belong now. That I feel like a citizen of, well, nowhere.

I reside in one place, I was born in another. I am not truly accepted anywhere, especially in this time of division and hatred towards non-whites. Where immigrant children are separated from their parents, where black people are shot walking down the street, kneed to death while cooperating with an officer or unable to deliver a package and held at gun point.

What kind of society are we living in now? How can we come together as a people and stop blaming others because you can't go get a drink at the bar? I am not Chinese, but even so, how are Chinese Americans responsible for a pandemic that started across the globe? This is nothing new. It has been bubbling under the surface since the beginning of time.

Since the Civil Rights movement. Since people are supposed to be "equal." I wish I had an answer but unfortunately those who are the perpetuators, this will fall on deaf ears. Still, especially for whites reading this, we need your help! We need to let others know this is not okay. It is not acceptable.

I ask for the support of my Caucasian brothers and sisters to help fight racism and to my fellow Asians: keep your head up. Be proud of who you are and spread awareness about our experiences so we can all come together as a people and those perpetuating hate can become the vast minority.

Bio

Jenelle Anderson was adopted at 18 months from Seoul, South Korea into a Caucasian family. She lived in Washington state until they moved to Central Oregon where she lived for the next 32 years (with a two year break in Portland). Jenelle received her Bachelors degree at Oregon State University in Liberal Studies and Sociology, followed by her Master of Adult Education. Passionate about helping people succeed and live full and self-determined lives, Jenelle worked as a direct support provider and adult education instructor. She has also worked as an office manager and now as a case manager for people who experience developmental disabilities. She lives with her husband, amazing rescue dog, cat and chickens. She spends her free time caring for her animals, gardening, reading fiction and researching topics of interest. She also loves to visit places in Oregon, especially the coast and the Wallowa mountains. Living in a small town has always appealed to Jenelle as she feels safer and likes a more laid back style of living.

Lisa Chau

Lisa Chau Haiku

Don't hate me
I am American, too
Just like you

Lisa Chau

Lisa Chau

Contact Info

Linkedin.com/in/**LisaChau** || (347) 394 - 7868

Creating compelling narratives to showcase entrepreneurial leadership

https://CloverCanal2020.wordpress.com

* NPR: http://wypr.org/post/marketing-trends-social-media-and-millennials

* US News & World Report: http://www.usnews.com/topics/author/Lisa_Chau

* Huffington Post: http://m.huffpost.com/us/author/Lisa-Chau

* Buzzfeed: https://www.buzzfeed.com/lisa03755

* Change Creator: https://changecreator.com/how-a-bootcamp-for-entrepeneurs-propelled-new-challenges-for-this-soloproneur

* Be Moving Forward: https://www.bemovingforward.com/Lisa-Chau

* Thrive Global: https://medium.com/thrive-global/c-a-n-a-l-5-essential-strategies-for-sustainable-success-with-lisa-chau-ef6651e4e1e4

* TED Talk: http://ed.ted.com/lessons/networking-for-the-networking-averse-Lisa-Green-Chau

* SXSW 2018 https://schedule.sxsw.com/2018/events/PP80193

Alejandro Ayala III

My Story

Hello AAA. My name is Alejandro Ayala III. I was introduced to you guys by a member of the AHN Hyun Martin.

For starters, I would like to say that I love you guys. I'm telling you this because in today's world, love is a very precious commodity. I feel like it's our responsibility to share this gift with everyone...just don't forget to love yourself too. For some that's a day to day struggle but you can't love anyone else if you can't love yourself.

With that being said, here's my story...

At the age of 16, I was kicked out of my parents house because I threatened to expose my father's dark secret which involved him cheating on my mother...so I've pretty much been on my own since then. To survive, I clung to friends or anyone that was willing to provide me with somewhere warm to lay my head.

As a youth, I walked miles on end to find work at different temp agencies in the city to make ends meet. At the time, minimum wage was only $5.15 so saving money was damn near impossible. Without a good moral compass in my life, I decided to turn to a life of crime. I started out selling weed, the crack, then morphine as well as weapons and anything that had street value. I did that for years until I lost a very good friend due to gang violence. I also nearly lost my life on four separate occasions and each time involved looking down the barrel of a loaded gun.

After I turned my back on that lifestyle, I decided to further my education in hopes of making something of myself. During that time I became a certified pharmacy technician (how ironic) and I also obtained my associates in social science. Before I could complete my education, my girlfriend at the time became pregnant...so instead of finishing college, I dropped out to work full time to provide us with a place to stay.

She and I got married months before our first son was born and we finally moved into an apartment that we would temporarily call home. She and I were close friends for 3 years prior to dating. After 1 year of dating, I proposed because I truly believed that she was one for me but...I found out later that I was so wrong. She ended up being a very abusive and emotionally unstable person. She didn't just abuse me and take advantage of the fact that I don't believe in hitting women in anger, but she also abused our children.

After a very long 9 year custody battle, I was finally awarded physical custody. Within those 9 years I used my book, common and street knowledge to not only land the great day job I have today, but I also own 2 properties and my own business. I juggle these responsibilities all while raising my 2 boys. I've also had the pleasure of working with several big names in the entertainment industry thanks to my talent for writing songs and screenplays.

Now...I feel like the time is right to share my story with the world.

Asian Hustle Network, I am currently seeking animators to help create an animated music video to bring one of my many stories to life. If YOU are an animator, I would love to see a sample of your work in hopes of doing business with you.

Please feel free to leave a link to your work in the comments section below or you can email me at louiethirteen@gmail.com.

Thank you again AHN for allowing me to share this little piece of myself with all of you. I believe that through our shared experiences we grow, we evolve and become stronger.

#LetsGrowTogether #DreamBigWorkHard

Bio

A Ali is an American songwriter, screenwriter and producer that hails from Portsmouth, Virginia. Due to A Ali's diverse Asian, African, Latin and Native American background, he never felt accepted by his peers as a youth which led to his love of music and the arts.

"Music was my escape from it all. My parents were poor so we didn't have a lot of things that other people had. We were living on Section 8 so on top of looking different from most kids that I went to school with, I didn't really have all of the designer clothes or shoes that most kids had so that was another thing that kind of made people distance themselves from me. I paid it no mind for the most part because I was there to learn but kids can be cruel which is why I chose music as an escape."

At age 5, Ali nearly lost his life to an unknown gunman while assisting his great grandmother with folding clothes on her back porch in the Swanson Holmes apartment complex in Portsmouth, Virginia.

"It was the projects so what can you say? Also, crack cocaine had just made a major impact in the area so it was a crazy time. I remember a guy in a trench coat running up to another guy that was standing a few steps away from me and moments later, he shot him in the head. My grandmother went inside for a sec before all of this happened because she had a customer come to the back door to buy some candy. She was the neighborhood's candy lady so she sold candy and icebergs. But yeah...it was one of those things you don't forget. Afterwards, I remember my great grandmother pulling me into the apartment and wiping my face and asking me if I was alright."

Unfortunately, this wouldn't be the last time Ali witnessed such a horrific act. Due to a falling out with his dad, Ali decided to run the streets and live a life of crime in hopes of making a name for himself and making enough money to make his dreams come true.

"When I found out my hero...my own father was cheating on my mom among other things, it really messed me up in the head. I was young and filled with so much hatred and resentment towards him. My moral compass was nonexistent at that time so naturally, I looked for guidance and belonging elsewhere."

But ultimately, this led to a downward spiral that nearly claimed his life.

"I saw a lot...did a lot...and thankful I survived it all because a lot of people didn't. I almost lost my life a few times...not to mention my freedom and everything I held dear. When something like that happens, you either wake up and you start to put certain things into perspective or you get caught up and never make it out of the rabbit hole. I wanted to live so I did what I had to do to survive."

Upon his awakening, Ali decided to make his passion for writing his top priority which led to key opportunities that further confirmed that writing was in fact his true calling. Opportunities such as creating the first theme song Welcome To BlackPlanet for the website BlackPlanet once it was acquired by Radio One in 2012 as well as having one of his songs featured on a movie entitled Sucker For Love which is currently featured on Amazon Prime.

"Everyone used to tell me that they loved my poetry and the way I expressed myself on paper but the moment you hear or see your work on a platform for everyone to see...that really solidified things and kind of let me know that I was on the right path."

After ghostwriting for numerous artists in the industry, Ali currently owns his own private recording studio in Midlothian, Virginia and has plans to release three new singles in 2021.

"Life is too short to take for granted. That's one thing the streets taught me. I just hope my story can help someone else turn their life around because there were so many moments where I thought it was too late. There were so many times where I wanted to give up but as long as you have breath in your body...it's never too late."

Alejandro Ayala III

Sarama Keum Sun

The Good, the Bad, and the Jack-A-Double S

John Wayne taught me to fight.

My father, however, taught me, "Sticks and stones may break my bones, but words will never hurt me."

I objected. "No! But it does hurt. He shouldn't say mean things to me. I didn't do anything to him."

I collapsed my folded elbows on the table in a huff, my chin resting on crossed wrists, scowling. We sat around the small kitchen table that straddled the divide between the coarse yellow-brown carpet of the living room, and the beige vinyl of the alley kitchen, a single bulb lighting our faces from above.

My father shrugged his freckly white shoulders. "Tell those kids," he answered, "that you were born in this country, and you're American, just like they are. Tell them that your dad is white."

My mother, her almond eyes trained patiently on my father's as she waited for his decree, accepted his judgment with a nod. Because she had immigrated as an adult, her childhood experience was vastly different. She did not know to expect that her daughter would experience racism. Instead, she would ask, her dark-olive face knit with concern, if the other children teased me for being poor. Which they did—but that was the least of my worries being that the other low-income children also rejected me for my ethnicity

"Tell them," was her advice, "that your grandfather was great man. Rich. So rich he built a church! But war took his money. Tell them!

Okay? Let them know!"

Tell them, said my mother, that under different circumstances you would have been something other than who you are—something more deserving of respect. Tell them, said my father, that the American half of you makes the other half palatable.

In second grade I was a little girl in black pigtails and plastic-framed glasses who played alone at recess. He was a little boy with brown hair and blue eyes, his puffy blue jacket contrasting with his pale complexion. The first time we had passed on the playground, his eyes lit up with such delight I thought I finally had a friend. The boy laughed gleefully, and from then on I had company every single afternoon recess.

He was from a different class so I didn't know his name, but he was certain mine was either "Ching-ching-China," or "Chink." He would run up, pulling back his eyes while babbling in imitation of Asian languages, and shout, "Go back to your country!"

I tried, "I am not Chinese; I am Korean," and "I was born in this country so this is my country," but those arguments did nothing to undermine his complete confidence that I looked different, and those that look different do not belong here.

I tried, "Go away."

To which he would respond, "You go away. Go away to your country."

I tried, "You're stupid."

He would answer with, "I know you are, but what am I?"

This was an retort I could never use against him, since he wasn't the Gook; I was. Instinctively, I knew that, "White boy!" would not be considered an insult.

"Sticks and stones," my father repeated each time I complained.

I disagreed. "But he follows me the whole recess! I can't make him stop, and he won't leave me alone."

"Well, did you tell the teachers?"

I had. Several times. They only hushed me and sometimes walked away in the middle of my pleas. After all, it was 1992 and, according to my teachers, racism died in the 60s.

"Well, sometimes you have to fight your own battles," my father replied.

Sometimes, he meant, no one will care enough to come to your aid.

No matter what tactics I used, the little boy remain undeterred in his torment. Gradually, I stopped fighting and tried to continue with my recess activities. I slunk around the playground, swung on the swings, while my companion followed a few feet behind, shouting and making faces. I came to accept his constant taunting shadow as though he were my conscience on my shoulder—an internal voice who found everything about my heritage morally repulsive. This harassment went on for several weeks, until the night I met John Wayne.

It was an hour or two after bedtime and I had woken up with a burning thirst. I padded half-asleep down a dark hall cushioned with silence to the kitchen for a glass of water. The end of the hall ahead was lit with dancing blue light. I emerged into the living room and, startled by the crack of a loud gunshot, bumped into the kitchen table at my right. On the glowing television set, a black-and-white John Wayne stood across from a crumpled figure, and with a derisive sneer, he barked, "Jackass."

"Jackass." The word filled my ears and tingled my brain with awe. "Jackass." It was an entirely new word for me, and I didn't really know what it meant, but damn, did I like it.

"Go to bed!" said my dad, suddenly spotting me.

I did, my eyes shining. I had a new weapon.

"Jackass."

The next day at school I could not wait for the previously dreaded afternoon recess. I was excited to be called racial slurs. He reported as usual, poor little dummy, with his usual litany. I didn't let him get very far. With pigtails pointed steadily to the ground and eyes scrunched behind my glasses, I spread my legs in a crouch, planted both feet, and with a ricochet motion of my torso for the most sound projection, I bellowed in my best John Wayne impression: "JACK-AAAASSS!"

I was nervous: maybe my weapon wouldn't work. Would he know what a "jackass" was? I didn't. Could you be hurt by a word you didn't understand? Maybe the boy would simply laugh. Maybe he would say, "I know you are but what am I?"

The boy's chubby cheeks scrunched and his face crumpled in an explosion of tears.

I was shocked. He had never reacted like that before. For a moment, I was concerned that I had badly hurt him. But on the heels of those two emotions was triumph. The sensation of power filled my chest as, bawling and wailing, he fled.

Right to the teacher.

I was immediately surrounded by chastising women. Where before they had looked at me with indifference, now they looked at me with dark judgment. The feeling of power burst and sunk to the ground, coming to rest in a puddle at my feet.

I was punished. I argued that he had been calling me names like "Ching-ching-China" for weeks, but the teachers spoke over me. I had used a cuss word. And cuss words were very very bad and only used by very very bad people. So bad, my dad was called. He came to the school embarrassed and swore he had not taught me that term: it was the fault of John Wayne and would never happen again.

I was made to apologize to the little boy and sent home for the rest of the day. Whereupon I was sternly lectured by my father.

"Swear words," he said, "are always inappropriate."

"But what about, 'sticks and stones'?" I asked, snotty and hoarse from the many hours of crying.

"Swear words don't count," he answered. "If you want people to like you, you have to be nice."

"But I was nice!" I wailed.

The boy returned next recess. "Ha ha! You used a bad word and got in trouble, Ching-ching-China!"

I walked away and he followed, jeering and taunting.

"What are you going to do about it? Huh? Go back to your country?"

I knew now there was nothing I could do but accept his torment. "Sticks and stones." I held to my father's words with a desperate grip. "Sticks and stones."

But underneath my father's voice was another: a voice that was new, confused, and unsure. But despite its hesitancy, it spoke in a determined, loud whisper. As the boy and I tread across the playground, this internal conscience peered backwards over my shoulder and sneered,

"Jackaaaasss.

Sarama Keum-Sun with her mom

Veronica Li

The American Choir, an Essay

My best friend at Sequoia High was a blind boy named Ken. He was tall as a beanpole, had a narrow, intense face, and sang a heart-wrenching tenor in perfect pitch. I was the new kid in school, having just immigrated with my family from Hong Kong. Ken and I met at the school choir and became friends during our travels to other school districts for competitions. On these trips, there was plenty of down time between performances.

The kids hung out in cliques, chitchatting, laughing, joking, which confirmed my impression from watching Hollywood movies that Americans were a big-hearted, fun-loving bunch. How I wanted to be a part of that scene. I tried to insert myself into one of the soprano groups, but quickly found that the beautiful harmony we shared ended the moment we left the stage. I was fifteen, an FOB still smelling of the sea, and trying desperately to fit in.

I scoured the room for someone to latch on to. Ken was sitting alone. Since he couldn't see me coming, I sidled up, so as not to startle him, and introduced myself. I didn't want to spell out that I was Chinese, but I did say I came from Hong Kong. We discovered we had much in common—love of music and literature, and we were both outcasts. One day, he asked me if I could record Gulliver's Travels for him. It was required reading in English class, and his fingers were getting worn out from reading Braille. I responded with enthusiasm, and the school supplied the taping equipment.

I took the recorder home and religiously read several chapters a day.

The next week, Ken had the entire Gulliver's Travels in audible format. Days later, I saw Ken in the cafeteria and approached him. Then I heard him say to the person beside him, "Boy, does she have an accent! I can't understand what she's reading."

I retreated, mortified. I might be able to mask my accent in casual conversations, but when it came to reading for hours on end, my choppy Chinese-British brogue camethrough loud and clear. I never read for Ken again. We remained friends until graduation and have since lost touch.

The year was 1967, the place San Francisco Bay Area. My family was among the first wave of immigrants taking advantage of the 1965 Immigration and Nationality Act. For the first time, the U.S. government allowed people outside of Northern Europe to legally immigrate to the U.S. The rich diversity of voices in the American choir today owes its origin to this law.

Since then, I've experienced other incidents that made me feel "less than" for any number of reasons: my race, gender, accent, youth (wish I still have it), or size. But these slights no longer devastate me. My skin has grown thick as a pachyderm's, and most importantly, the longer I wear it, the more comfortable I feel in it, like a favorite T-shirt that one hates to change out of. I've become very much at home with my hyphenated identity—a Chinese who values certain old-world traditions, and an American who appreciates this land is built by immigrants like myself and those who came before me. I thought nothing could shake me up, but the following encounter did.

Sometime in early March 2020, I was at a pharmacy anxiously looking for hand sanitizers. The store was on the Eastern Shore of the Chesapeake Bay, where I have a vacation home by the water. I was on my way there from my primary residence in Northern Virginia, and the plan was to stock up on the essentials for coping with the COVID-19 pandemic. As I'd feared, I was too late. The shelves were empty. There was only one worker in the store, a woman who appeared to be a baby boomer like myself but must be younger than I since she was still working. She looked wiped out, her pasty face heavy with an expression that said, I don't want to be here! After I asked her when a new shipment of hand sanitizers was expected, she grunted an uninformative reply.

Then I asked for the next best, rubbing alcohol, and her answer was the same.

Fortunately, I found something more precious—toilet paper! I put some rolls in my basket and took them to the self-checkout register. The machine kept dinging at me. I asked for help and the woman told me to ignore it; that was just the way it worked. While I was paying, I overheard her talking to another shopper, telling him about a stupid customer who couldn't figure out the checkout machine. The words went in one ear and out another. I loaded my car and started driving home. Suddenly it dawned on me this stupid customer was me! She was talking about me, in a voice loud enough for me to hear! Was that intentional or did she think my English was so elementary that I couldn't understand her subtle slur?

I wanted to drive back and give her a piece of my mind. The Chinese side of me said, let it go, while the American side said, you can't let her get away with it. I ended up doing neither. Instead I stewed over it. What irked me most was that her insult was so insidious and indirect that I didn't have the chance to volley back. If she had yelled, "Go back to where you came from!"—an abuse directed at many Asian Americans these days, including three friends of mine—I would gladly have yelled back, "I'm an American! What are you? No American would say a thing like that!"

Her scoffing voice buzzed in my ears for a few days, but gradually it faded. Her broad, weary face hovered around instead. A softer feeling crept up in me and I realized it was sympathy. I came to this country with nothing; she was born and raised here at the height of American prosperity. Here I am fifty years later, sheltering in two homes, while she's sent to the front line as cannon fodder. The modern global economy has left her behind, and I don't fault her for being mad. But why take it out on me? Because it's easy to blame people who look different, especially when certain political leaders goad you on.

I won't apologize for taking my piece of the American pie, but I also understand we're all members of the same choir. If there's a bright side to the pandemic, it's the highlighting of our interdependence regardless of race or class. We're all in trouble when COVID-19 batters workers at meat-packing plants and essential store clerks such as the one who snubbed me. Next time I go to the pharmacy, I'll look for her and thank her for the service she's doing for us all.

Bio

Two and a half years in an American public school changed my life forever. I was fifteen when I arrived at Sequoia High in Redwood City, California. It was 1967, the year my parents took my four siblings and me to the U.S. so that we could have the best college education. Before then, we had been living mostly in Hong Kong.

Having traveled half the world to go to school, I dived right away into my studies. To my shock and horror, I discovered that in an American public school, a student's popularity was in inverse proportion with his grades. Being a foreigner and straight A go-getter, I was an outcast. My social life consisted of hanging out with teachers after school and doing extra-credit work (which endeared me to my classmates even more). One teacher who always kept an open door was Mrs. Bradley, my English teacher. On the pretext of discussing books, I went to her after school every day. It should have come as no surprise that I majored in English at U.C. Berkeley. After graduating, journalism became the outlet for my urge to write. I went to work for the Hong Kong office of AFP, the French news agency. In 1976, when the Asian Wall Street Journal started operations in Hong Kong, I joined the young and dynamic pioneer staff. It was a privilege to participate in the birth of a newspaper.

Two years later, personal and career factors led me to enroll in graduate studies at the School of Advanced International Studies of Johns Hopkins University. Living in D.C. where the school was located, I had the opportunity to intern at the State Department. After obtaining my master's degree in International Affairs, the World Bank hired me as a Young Professional, the title for a management-track recruit. At the time, China had just become a member of the World Bank. My Chinese proficiency was an advantage.

For six years, I traveled to my home territory, East Asia, to assess Bank-financed development projects. In a spurt of adventurousness, I transferred to East Africa, specifically to work on Somalia. The excitement that awaited me went far beyond my expectations. I watched the country explode into civil war, some say despite western aid, others say because of it. The Somali tragedy moved me deeply, and I began searching for answers.

The old writing bug bit me. To understand something, I have to write about it. In 2000, when I was no longer with the World Bank, I published a spy thriller, Nightfall in Mogadishu, featuring an Asian American Jane Bond sent to save the failing country. My second book, Journey across the Four Seas, is about my mother's life. I wrote it after my elderly parents moved in with me. To take care of them, I needed to find out who they were. My third book, Confucius Says is a fictionalized tale of a Chinese American daughter's struggle to take care of elderly parents while caring for herself. For the first time, she reads Confucius in his own words and understands the true meaning of "honor your father and mother."

I now live in Northern Virginia. My latest book, of which I'm my husband's co-author, is *Viking Voyager: An Icelandic Memoir*. I'm also the author of *Journey across the Four Seas: A Chinese Woman's Search for Home and Confucius Says: A Novel.*

— www.veronicali.com.

Veronica Li

Anita Merina

Sometimes, the visual arts need no explanation.

#Racismisavirus

Metamorphosis

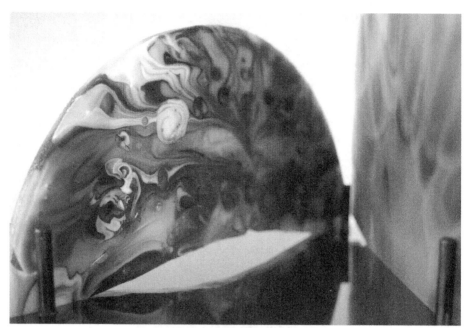

Nautilus

Peace

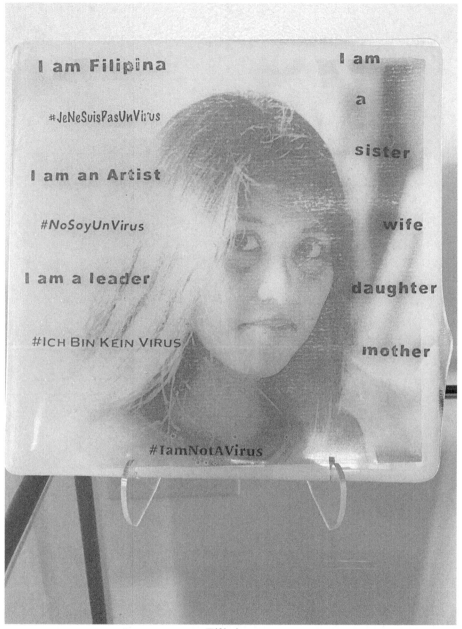

Filipina

A Mother's Lament, A Warrior's Cry

Before you were born
I carried your bodies in mine
And lay in bed for months
Resting so you'd see the light of day
I swaddled you both with soft cloth
Tucking the ends in
To make you feel safe
Like the womb that was your home
When the tornado came upon us
Out of a dark brown sky
I covered your bodies with mine
And shouted "I love you"
To drown out the sound of the freight train
And when a sniper threatened our city D.C.
Like many fearful parents
I walked alongside your skipping selves
Hunched over bracing for bullets that never came
In teen and college years
You knew too well to walk with purpose
Keys in hand
The middle of the street
The lighted path
But this, not this
A mother's love could not protect you
From this
The racist, leering comments
Cutting deep into you
The pattern
Of cat-calls, come-ons, threats of an assault
Even my own stories of survival
Could never prepare you, never protect you
So much pain,

Anita Merina

The pain of Asian women
Objectified, sexualized, traumatized
And the reality that some of us never make it
The terror of Atlanta, the overwhelming grief
The not being seen, not being heard
And so, I march with you
Calling upon our women warrior ancestors
To join us and to shield us in our solidarity
Amplify our voices and our rage
Let our rally cry ring loud inside their ears
Our voices, votes, and actions
Strike down the white supremacist
Root of never ending waves of hate
Against our sisters, brothers, children, elders
We cannot stop, we must not stop
And when you tire and tire you will
Let mama's love still comfort you
And help you rest until you rise again.

— © Anita Merina 2021

Pain and Power: A Message from an Asian American Mother

Before they were even born, my twin daughters were subjected to my fierce will to protect them. Ours was a high-risk pregnancy and I remained in bed for five months to ensure their survival. I then underwent an emergency C-section after 36 hours of labor.

When they were toddlers, I'd wheel the stroller into the middle of a soccer field to allow them to run free but also give me space to scoop up one and then run in the opposite direction to grab the other giggling runner.

When they were five and an unexpected tornado hit the University of Maryland as I was picking them up from the university's Center for Young Children, I held their bodies down with my own and shouted "I love you," as the tornado upended cars in the nearby parking lot and my daughter Tasiana cried, "What's happening?"

A year later, with the DC sniper still on the loose, I, like many parents in the DC area, shielded my twins' bodies as I walked them into their elementary school. I gave them my cell phone with instructions to call 911 as I filled my car up at the gas station, fearful of the DC sniper would strike again.

By the time they were through their teen and college years, they were armed with the knowledge of how to recognize signs of partner abuse, micro-aggressions, sexism and the importance of therapy. They also were inspired by examples of the strong Asian American women I'd worked both for and alongside, women politics, education, and activism. They knew the story of their Lola, my mother, who shielded her own children during the Japanese occupation of the Philippines. They learned how, during the lean years in the U.S., she ate miniscule portions of food so that her children would have enough to eat.

They even had their lessons in racism. How their Lola chased away the racist kids who threw rocks at us when we were playing in the driveway of our new California home. How the parents of my Japanese-American high school boyfriend met in the internment camps. How I didn't fully know the history of racism toward Filipinos and other Asian Americans until I went to UCLA. How DC elementary school parents thought I was their nanny and how a neighbor once asked if I could tap into the Filipino housemaid network for a friend and how, when he saw the look on my face, said, "Oh, I mean nurse." (Had he said Filipino mail order bride I would have hit the trifecta.). Their support of and solidarity with their BIPOC and LGBTQ peers is rooted in the racial profiling they experienced, witnessed, and called out.

And yet, nothing I could do or say could fully prepare or protect them for the trauma of today. The daily reports of anti-Asian violence both verbal and physical, the bullying and racist association with COVID, the attacks on elders who look like their late Lolo and Lola. The unpredictability of the attacks on sidewalk, bus stops, stores and shopping malls and schools.

And then there are Atlanta spa shootings. The murders of those Asian women and the reporting of that horrific event evoke the realities of objectification, sexualization and violence that are all too familiar to my daughters and to me. The racist comments and threats that immediately follow a rejection of advances. The stares and leering comments, the catcalls, the social media blasts, and the assaults on our bodies.

At least my daughters were able to share their experiences with me. As a two-time sexual assault survivor when I was a teen and later as a college student, were both rooted in the same objectification. I didn't share my trauma with authorities or even my own sisters until many years later and I never told my mother. They still haunt me to this day.

What my daughters continue to teach me is that we must speak out--loudly, forcefully, passionately, courageously. The daughters are teaching the mother! We know that for the thousands in the AAPI community who have filed reports of violence against them, thousands more, Asian American women in particular, stay silent in fear, in shame, and in trauma. We must continue to speak out for them. We can channel our own pain, our rage, our passion, into action. We must rally for their sake, for their survival. We cannot rest. We must speak out. And you....must listen. #StopAAPIHate

To learn how you can help stop anti-Asian American and xenophobic harassment, go to Asian Americans Advancing Justice, www.aajc.org and Hollaback! at www.hollaback.org

My Country 'Tis of Me

My country 'tis of me

My friends and family

Of thee I dream

Land of our cultural pride

Gone are the great divides

Throughout this countryside

Let freedom ring

My country 'tis of thee

True land of liberty

Of thee I sing

Freedom from hate and fear

Threats against those I hold dear

May all our rights be clear

Let freedom ring

My country 'tis of thee

Telling our history

Of this I dream

Heroes who look like us

Stories in class to discuss

Teachers who know this a plus

Of this I dream

My country 'tis of thee

Sweet land of liberty

Of thee I sing

My Country 'Tis of Me

Land where we're truly free

All who look just like me

Be who we want to be

Let freedom ring

©Anita Merina, all rights reserved

Bio

Anita Merina (she/her) is a Filipino-American writer and literacy advocate. She is working on a book about Victoria Manalo Draves, a Filipino-American diver who overcame racism to win two Olympic Gold medals in 1948. She is also at work on a memoir, This I Can Tell You, dedicated to daughters Tasiana and Corina.

Anita Merina is a writer and glass artist based in Deal Island, Maryland. She is National Board Chair of the Little Free Library organization and a longtime advocate for diverse books and amplifying Asian American voices in particular. A Filipina-American, she is the daughter of immigrants, both parents from Batanes, the northernmost province in the Philippines.

Anita Merina

Alice Stephens

Origin Story

She carefully tied the ribbon of her best hanbok, the silk slipping through her trembling fingers as she fumbled to tie the complicated bow. Then she turned to the mirror that he had found for her at a flea market, the edges scalloped with rot, her pale, serious face framed by it. She slowly brushed her thick hair, arranging it just so to hide that her stylish hair-cut needed a trim. Carefully plucking two bobby pins from a tray made from the lid of a Band-Aid tin, she tucked the unruly hair neatly behind her ears.

The soft bundle that lay on a matt on the floor briefly pulsed with movement but then was still again.

She would not put on lipstick, she didn't want the official to think she was a cheap bar girl. Though they never married, they lived together for 13 months. She cooked, cleaned and cared for him, just like a real wife. And he took all the prerogatives of a husband.

She did, however, dust her face lightly with rice powder. She came from the countryside, and her cheeks had a ruddy glow that betrayed the years she spent working in the sun. Americans didn't care about whiteness though. To them, you were already foreign, whether you had the luminescent moon-glow of Young Mee or the caramel luster of Ji Soo, whose mother was rumored to be from the Philippines. A gook was a gook. But she was his gook.

A soft mewl emanated from the swaddling on the floor, a light kiss of noise in the hot air.

Very sparingly, she dabbed on some rouge, the powder now but a thin ring rimming the edge of the compact. Finally, she skirted the bundle of white on the floor to take a gold ring from a pouch hidden in the very back of her closet. She softly stroked the simple gold band before sliding it onto her finger. She realized now that she should have known he wasn't coming back when he gave her the ring. It was not a promise that he would return for her, as she had originally thought, but a parting gift, something that could be converted to cash if times got desperate enough.

Well, times were desperate now.

She kissed a fingertip and touched it to the frayed edge of a small sketch of her face. It was all she had left of him, a drawing that he had made of her. There had once been a photograph of them together, hand in hand. But in an act of desperation, she had sent it to the address he left as a good faith gesture, to remind him that she was still here, still in the same condition that he'd left her in, and if he didn't send for her soon, she'd have to take matter into her own hands.

A little dramatic, she knew, but drama was the only weapon she had left.

He was neither moved nor shamed into responding. She had waited as long as she could for him. Bending as she used to in the rice fields, she gathered the small bundle from the floor, nestling it into a crooked arm. At the doorway, she guided her feet into silk embroidered shoes and then stepped out into the narrow alleyway.

No one was about except for a gutter cat. They slunk past each other, she walking quickly to avoid the prying eyes of her neighbors. Turning onto the street, she cradled per package close to her bosom. She made it all the way to the bus station without meeting anyone she knew.

A man gallantly gave her a seat on the bus, and she thought if he knew what she was holding in her arms, he wouldn't have been so polite. But her mind, with the nimbleness of a gazelle dodging a predator, swerved away from the errand that lay ahead, and instead she lost herself in watching other people: a chubby cheeked toddler sitting like an emperor on his mother's lap, she knock-kneed to keep him from falling between her legs; three schoolgirls in shabby uniforms and socks sagging at the ankles, their youth so painful she had to look away; an aged couple with hands folded in the same prayer-like way against their chests.

Lots of people got off at her stop. She swayed in the restless current of the crowd for a moment before stopping a grandmotherly type with a humped back and tortured gait for guidance. Pointed in the right direction, she joined the flow of pedestrians, arms crossed and shoulders hunched as she held her bundle close.

At the imposing glass doors, she paused for a moment. It was a typical August day, the heat clinging like a plastic film, and she was bathed in sweat. The door swung open and a man beckoned her in. "That way," he said, nodding towards a long corridor that disappeared into the distance. "Third door on the right."

Her sweated skin turned clammy, and she was deathly cold and burning hot at the same time. The man bowed encouragingly. "Go ahead."

One foot in front of another, she proceeded past the man. But then her knees wouldn't stop bending and she had to stop to regain control of her shaking legs. The bundle in her arm began to shift and warp, as if there were something alive in there.

There was something alive in there. Jiggling her arm, the woman resumed walking, the quick tapping of her best shoes echoing down the empty corridor. She paused at a door, her jiggling more frantic, before opening it just as the bundle began to bleat and squirm.

The nurse's apron was so stiff with starch that it crackled as she held her arms out. Hastily, the woman parted the cocoon of cotton that swaddled the baby she was holding.

She kissed my cheek and let me go.

On the Anniversary of My Orphanhood

August 2nd is an anniversary of sorts for me: the date on which I became an orphan, a mere seven days after I was born.

In reality, I was an orphan on paper only. I had a Korean mother who was alive, who had given me away with her own flesh-and-blood hands. I had an American GI father who knew about my imminent arrival and fled.

I have a copy of that paper that declares me an orphan. It is of translucent onion skin, stamped with a vermilion-inked seal that sealed my fate. I regarded that document as a testament to my mother's love for me: fragile, flimsy, easily torn. The kind of love that made it possible to declare her own child an orphan.

As I grew up, I gave little thought to my birth mother. She had relinquished me to the comfort of strangers. *They* were my family now. She had had her chance to be my mother, and had passed on it. Passed me on.

Besides, I had my own problems to worry about. I was kind of a messed up kid. I had the issues that come with being a dark-haired, slant-eyed face in a sea of white: low confidence, aversion to the spotlight, self-loathing, an unrequited and unrequitable yearning to fit in.

And yet, I thought I was smarter than most people, fearing the spotlight just a bit more than I craved it. I wanted people to admire me, to acknowledge that, despite my failure to be white, I was better, sharper, faster than they were.

So, naturally, I decided to be a writer. Actually, even before I became consumed by my identity issues, writing was my only ambition. But my early attempts were hollow—everything I wrote was ersatz white; it had no soul. In order to become the kind of writer I wanted to be, one who wrote literary fiction that profoundly pondered upon the mystery of the human condition, I had to probe the mystery of me.

Painfully aware of the sacrifice that my Korean mother had made, my American mother encouraged me to look for her. As a gesture to my mother, I inquired with my adoption agency. When they mentioned a hefty fee to start the search process, I balked. Why should I pay to find the woman who had sent me halfway across the world in order to rid herself of me?

But it wasn't really the money. My adoptive mother offered to pay for the fee. Subconsciously I knew that before I could search for my Korean mother—or write the great American novel—I had to heal the broken places that existed within myself. With the help of a patient and loving partner, I faced the anger and confusion that had roiled me for so long. I learned to love myself for who I was, and not who I wanted to be.

Of course, the question of my origins has been an ever present haunting. From whom did I get my thick earlobes? My broad shoulders and slender build? My freckles and moles? The red highlights in my hair? When doctors ask about my medical history, I have none to give. The older I get, the more I realize I am being cheated of a right to know the basic facts about my own body.

After my kids left for college and my debut novel was accepted for publication, I took a DNA test to find out what exactly comprised the half of me that wasn't Korean. Because of those freckles and red highlights—and a fondness for drink and potatoes—I guessed I was part Irish. That's how white-washed I was: it never occurred to me that my American half wasn't Caucasian.

Turns out, I now have a few more boxes to check on race and

ethnicity surveys. I am 20% Native American from the southern region of what is now Mexico, 15% Iberian, and a smattering of everything else (including a smidgen of Neanderthal). I have always said that I'm a citizen of the world, and it's true. I really am.

My DNA also matched me to hundreds of relatives, including someone who was a first cousin or closer. Here was a chance to find out about my birth father, maybe even meet him. I hesitated long and hard to contact this close relative before deciding that I was strong enough to survive a worst case scenario. As a purveyor of stories, I had an obligation to find out my own.

I will never meet my birth father because he died years ago. At least now I know to get annual skin checks from my dermatologist for melanoma. And I see who bequeathed me my unruly, coppery hair and fat earlobes. Surprisingly, I have his eyes like scalene triangles with saggy long vertexes. My oldest son has his Aztec nose.

I met his son, my half-brother, and a week later, my debut novel was published. I do not think the timing was a coincidence.

It is doubtful that my Korean mother is still alive. According to the (frequently unreliable) information from the adoption agency, she was 35 when she made me an orphan. Her life since then has likely been a hard one. At 35, she would have been old to return to the bar girl life.

I had long known that she gave me up to spare me from a life of discrimination in South Korea, but I know now just how institutionalized that discrimination was. I've also learned about the South Korean government's facilitation of prostitution around American base camps and the systematization of exportation of unwanted mixed-race babies for adoption to white, wealthy nations, which eventually grew to include the "pure-blooded" children of desperately poor married couples, and indeed, paved the way for the transnational adoption industry that has since flourished.

By declaring me an orphan, my birth mother erased herself from history. By searching for her, I am taking the truth back.

Things You Have Touched

What do I have of yours?

Of what you have touched:

1. A piece of tissue-thin onion-skin paper to which you pressed your vermilion-inked seal, and so sealed my fate. Belying the fragility of the parchment, it is an iron-clad document that "releases" me—as if I were a prisoner or a caged animal—from the mother who wanted me and the motherland that did not, to cross the great, roiling ocean to call another, "Mother."

2. Three photos hidden in the attic of my birth father's recently deceased half-sister, sent to me by a half-brother I have only just met. You must have taken the photos after you relinquished me at two weeks old, for in them I am not a scaly, blind-eyed newborn but a real human being who could look at the camera, and into the future, with startled and wary eyes. You sent these photos to my birth father hoping that he would come back to claim me, to claim us, slipping them into a tear-stained (this is an embellishment that I cannot help, as I am a writer—*did you make me a writer?*) envelope which has long ago been discarded.

    a. One photograph I had seen already, affixed to the emigration travel document issued by the Republic of Korea. It has always been my equivalent of baby's first photo, the one that usually gets taken in the hospital ward, a swaddled baby in a hospital-issue cap being cradled in a proud parent's arms. I am bare-headed, my hair already wild and unruly, and laying in no one's arms.

    b. In the next one, I am in someone's extended arms (*yours?*), just a glimpse of bare skin between rolled-up sleeves and the pillow of cloth on which I lay like Cinderella's glass slipper. *Do I fit you? Or you? Who will take me home?* I look strange in this photo, like a Kabuki baby with two dots for lips and a patch of white around my mouth. Lolling back on my litter, I look at the camera with an air of pampered ennui. Time has degraded all the photos, but this one the most, the black fading into a reflective silvery sheen, ghostly and haunted.

c. The third one is my favorite. Same roly-poly baby, same bedding, but in tighter focus and better lighting. The condition of the photo, now an ancient artifact, is good as well, the black still a black that absorbs and not a black that reflects. The light plays off the intricate folds of my loose clothing with the gleaming richness of a Vermeer or the luster of a Velázquez. But it is not the image that makes me value this photo above the others, it is what appears on the back in a scrawl of blue ink. Maybe it's not your handwriting, but they are your words. The only words of yours I've ever known. Words as intangible as love. Words that mean nothing and everything. Words that simultaneously break and heal my heart: "When daughter lay down picture cheeks. I thought that daughter is a bigest (sic) baby and face is also like your face. Korea 67".

3. Finally: my body. When I touch myself, I am touching you. But the skin that you once stroked has long ago been sloughed off; those "picture cheeks" are time-stippled and withered. I used to look at my face, my body, and wonder what is mine, what is yours, what is ours? Now I look and I wonder, *Are you still alive?*

The Villain in My Story

It is human nature to make sense of the world by creating stories. Where did we come from? Why are we here? For most, the fundamental questions of our own origins are already answered. I come from my mother and father, who came from their mother and father, and unto perpetuity.

But as an adoptee, I had to construct my own origin story. That story has evolved over time to accommodate my changing understanding of the world, and as I gradually comprehended the enormity of what it meant to be adopted. This compulsive arrangement and rearrangement of the scant few facts of my birth into a coherent narrative is, I am convinced, the reason I became a writer.

Most children have photo albums, scrap books and keepsake journals of their first days, weeks, and months of life. The proud parents showing off their newborn for the camera. The tiny, inky foot print. The official birth certificate adorned with a seal. The birth announcement reporting the precise details of weight, length, and time of birth.

As an adoptee, I have The File.

The File contains documents related to my parents' effort to adopt me, from their initial correspondence that began shortly after the birth of their third child to my U.S. naturalization papers issued when I was four years old.

The File also offers the earliest photo of me, a big-headed baby with a handsome shock of hair, staring with trepidation into the camera, and into a future that would take me far away from my birth mother and her home country. When I look at it, I see an Asian baby, but my fellow Koreans saw only the Caucasian in me. On the Korean Social Services, Inc. (KSS), case-study intake form, it is noted that I'm big for my age with a fair complexion and eyes that are "large and Caucasian-shaped."

Tell that to all the kids who pulled their eyes at me while screeching nonsensical sounds they thought sounded Chinese.

Everything I know about my biological parents and the circumstances of my birth is in that three-page document. But there is a hot-blooded, human story that lay underneath the cold, clinical statements.

Adoption stories are unreliable. One must depend upon official records, which are not always accessible, and hearsay, vague rumor and word-of-mouth. The first version of my adoption story had me abandoned on a doorstep, a simple way to communicate to a very young me that my birth mother had relinquished me. I spent years picturing myself as a baby curled up in a cardboard box on a crumbling concrete doorstep, waiting for someone to discover me.

Actually, as the case-study form in The File makes clear, my birth mother didn't leave me outside, vulnerable and helpless like Oedipus on Mount Cithaeron, but handed me over to KSS in person.

It must have been humiliating to submit to the KSS interview, enduring the social worker's judgment of her as a cheap bar girl stuck with the just consequences of her shameful livelihood. But she acquitted herself well—the social worker described her as "a talkative, sociable and cheerful woman."

Other things I know about my birth mother from the case-study form: her name, hometown, and physical appearance (condescendingly described as "rustic"). The middle child of three, she married a school teacher when she was 22 and left him four years later because he abused her, a courageous act of defiance in patriarchal Korea. She held on to me for two weeks before surrendering me for adoption.

Here's the reason why she felt obliged to give me up: "Recognizing her difficulty in providing care for the baby because of her limited financial situation and the baby's different coloring and appearance, she has decided to release her baby for adoption abroad."

She very rightfully feared for me as a mixed-race child in a society that considers themselves their own glorious, distinct, pure-blooded race. Discrimination against multi-racial Koreans is well documented, and I would have likely endured a life of bullying, social ostracism and diminished economic opportunities.

Defying the strict conventions of a rigid, male-dominated society that preferred she stay with a husband who beat her, she was no coward. She was a survivor, and she wanted me to survive too.

She was 35, an advanced age for a bar girl, and was not local to my birthplace of Uijeongbu, the village that had grown into a city thanks to the Cold War. Her family was from Gwangju in the south, but she fled from there to a place where a disgraced woman could make a living. The case study says, "Accordingly she began to associate with American soldiers and met the baby's father."

As The File attests, even official documents can bear false witness. In order for me to be given up for adoption, the South Korean bureaucracy demanded that I be declared an orphan, entering me in the *hoju* (official family registry) as the head—and sole member—of my own family, as if I had sprung from the earth whole, instead of from the womb of a Korean woman. The File holds the "Application for Certificate of Orphanhood" and a carbon copy of my *hojukdunbon* (family registration) which declared that my Father and Mother were Unknown, even when my mother's seal was stamped on the "Statement of Release for Emigration and Adoption Overseas."

Every adoption story has a villain. There was a reason why a mother, against the laws of nature, would give up a baby she has nurtured and sheltered with her own body for nine months. The most obvious culprit is the man who put her "in the family way," without offering her the family to go with it. By refusing to recognize his paternity, he turns the mother of his baby into a social pariah, preyed upon by mortified relatives, disapproving religious officiants, cruel gossiping neighbors and insurmountable bureaucratic obstacles. Society demands nothing less than the sacrifice of the fallen woman's baby on the altar of an unknown future. Total abandonment. Complete abdication of all maternal rights.

Most adoptees are told that they were surrendered as an act of love. In tacit acknowledgment that the birth mother is a victim of unjust social, legal and biological laws, adoptive parents typically depict her decision to give up her baby as one of reparation, not to be condemned but to be celebrated and cherished. *Her sacrifice brought you to us, to your life of privilege and plenty.* She may be pitied, but never reviled. I never thought of my birth mother as the antihero of my story.

From the sparse details presented in The File, it was my birth father who was the obvious villain. He enjoyed the privileges and pleasures of living with a woman who cooked, cleaned and let him have his way with her, which resulted in pregnancy, as sexual relations are known to do.

They lived together for 13 months. Common-law marriage, it said on the form.

Fully aware of her condition, he returned to the United States, likely promising to send for her. Why else would my birth mother hold on to me for two weeks?

I imagine my mother during that time, desperation mounting as the months passed with no news from him. He just left her to wait and wonder as her belly grew bigger and her savings smaller. She never heard another word from him.

He was the colonizer, she the colonized. And I am American hegemony in the flesh.

If my father had only faced up to the consequences of his actions, I would not have been separated from the woman who gave birth to me. I would be calling her *Mom*, instead of *my birth mother*. He could have saved us the anguish of separation.

If I felt anguish at the time, I don't remember it. (Never mind, the anguish came later. Not as a toddler or those golden years of early childhood, the much loved youngest child of four, the indulged baby of the family. But later, when I began to question my place within the society that I had always thought of as my own, and realized that I'd forever be on the outside looking in.) What does a baby know? One minute the warm, radiant center of your universe is holding you in the crook of her arm as you drink of her body, and the next she is gone.

Did I wail when I realized it was not she who held me but a stranger? I was put in foster care for nine months as my case wended its way through the bureaucratic labyrinth of two nations' migration and family laws. Did I balk at the unfamiliar arm that cradled me with a no-nonsense grip, and at the strange rubber nipple that was thrust into my mouth instead of soft, pliant flesh? I think I must have. That part of my story has never changed.

And I must presume that my mother missed me. From her life, came mine. We shared the most primal human connection possible. It must have been heartbreaking. Giving me up to save me. Not because she wanted to, but because she had to.

Here's what the form tells me about my villain: nationality, marital status (single), age (24), army rank (SP/4), and brief physical description (dark brown eyes and hair, fair complexion, sturdy, glasses).

And then, the story of their relationship in two brief sentences. Co-habitation, the date of his departure, and this: "After his return to the United States, she did not hear from him."

As The File clearly shows, my birth mother did the right thing and my birth father did not. He behaved in a contemptible and cowardly way. He used her up and threw her away. And he threw me away too.

A person can get a complex from that kind of shit.

Perhaps he joked about it with his army pals, taking the silver bird escape, getting the fuck out of Dodge at just the right moment. Of course he said he'd send for her. She was washing his underwear, cooking his meals, and saving him money on whores, so why wouldn't he lie to her up to the very end?

The year was 1967, the height of the Vietnam War. A working class boy, he enlisted in the army to make a better life for himself. By enlisting, he saved himself from combat duty.

Even though he was from a poor family, he had never seen poverty as it existed in South Korea in 1967. After decades of colonialism under the Japanese and a devastating war that literally tore the country into two, the fledgling nation was undergoing rapid industrialization but people still led mean, hardscrabble lives.

For the first time in his life, he felt rich and powerful, the White Conqueror among a bedraggled, hungry populace. Here, his army paycheck could stretch far; he could live like a Big Man, rent himself a house, find a comely woman willing to take care of it—and him—for nothing more than free room and board, a few baubles, and whispered promises of life in the Land of Opportunity.

Maybe he even felt a twinge of sorrow as his tour was ending. In the States, women wouldn't fawn over him as they did in Korea, where a guy goes to a bar and is instantly surrounded by a bevy of beautiful women, all begging for his attention. At home, you had to court a woman, she didn't court you. But that regret turned into relief every time he tried to tell her a joke but she didn't get it because her English wasn't good, or whenever she cooked with too much red pepper and garlic, or the times she scolded him for coming into the house with his shoes on. At night, as she welcomed his embraces, he really did mean it when he promised to send for her. But in the light of day, he knew he'd never send for her, despite the baby. Because of the baby.

He couldn't take them back home. His family wouldn't welcome them. Mother and baby would stand out in his small, redneck town. He couldn't face the shame.

And after all, he told himself, that was life during wartime. He took his manly spoils and what happened in Korea stayed in Korea.

But as I learned more about history, the responsibilities of government, and the deeply ingrained biases that shape national laws, I began to feel a strange sympathy for my villain. He was but a product of his time (and I the byproduct). He was a shining white knight in a sea of yellow, the conquering hero who took his small rewards for his patriotic sacrifice for his country. His villainy was but a microcosmic example of his country's villainy. He was just doing his bit for American expansionism.

Perhaps, too, my birth mother shared some of the blame. Desperate to go to America because at 35 she was aging out of her career as a bar girl, she may have become pregnant on purpose as a last ditch bid, an all-or-nothing gamble.

She lost that gamble, and was left with nothing, not even her child. Her society would not allow her to keep it. Her government conspired to get rid of it.

And here I discovered another, more implacable, villain. Since the Korean War, South Korea has exported over 200,000 children, mostly to the US. Instead of promoting changes that would result in less unwanted babies and a cultural acceptance of illegitimate offspring, the government set up meticulous regulations that imparted a veneer of careful oversight into what was, essentially, baby trafficking. Not for profit, but simply as a convenient way to get rid of the unwanted dregs of society in a tight economy.

But if South Korea is to be blamed, so must America, who waged war in countries that were entitled to their own sovereignty, and didn't do enough to prevent their troops from leaving behind their bastard children.

It was almost inevitable that my birth father would do what he did. It would take a real hero to claim his half-breed baby and bring her and her mother home. He was no hero, but he wasn't a dastardly villain either. He was just an ordinary man.

After taking a DNA test, I must now amend my origin story once again to incorporate yet another twist in the plot. The only truth I know for sure is that my life is a fiction. Yours probably is as well.

The Kindness of Strangers

An adoptee returning home from a trip back to my birth land, I had a lot to unpack. Literally. Along with my dirty clothes and souvenirs, there were the gifts that had been given to me during my eleven day stay in South Korea. My suitcase was bulging with them: books, elegant china mugs, colorful paddle fans, fine examples of local linen work...

The gift that I most treasure is a rather odd one, a framed cutting of a few rusty inches of DMZ barbed wire, given by the city of Paju, a town that was home to many U.S. military camps and the women who provided services to them.

The story of modern Korea is one of separation, the north from the south, siblings from siblings, mothers from their children. A pawn of history, it is a country on whom the Cold War is indelibly written, broken into two by the rivalries of empires both neighboring and distant.

I, too, am a product of the Cold War, a child born of the union of an American serviceman and a local woman. I, too, have been separated from my blood relatives.

Transnational adoption began with mixed-race children like me. Patriarchal Korean society had no place for bastard children of polluted blood, and enormous societal and bureaucratic pressure was put on women to relinquish their half-breed kids. Meanwhile, American organizations like the one through which I was adopted, Welcome House, considered it only right and just that American families take in these children that were, after all, half-American. When the Korean government saw how successful intercountry adoption was in getting rid of their unwanted children, they expanded the enterprise to include full-blooded Koreans. Approximately 200,000 Korean-born adoptees have been adopted out of the country.

Despite our designation as orphans, the vast majority of Korean adoptees had living parents at the time of their adoptions. I had a mother who held onto me for two weeks, hoping my birth father, a man with whom she had a thirteen-month relationship, would return to claim me. Even after she turned me over to the orphanage, she mailed him photos of me, noting on the back of one how much I resembled him.

Finally, she had to let me go. Her country gave her no choice. As an illegitimate child, I could not be entered in the national family registry, which at the time required a male head of household. Without a family registry, I was essentially persona non grata in my own land, ineligible for all public services such as they existed back then in a desperately poor country. My birth mother knew I would face a lifetime of prejudice and discrimination, vastly diminishing my prospects for success or happiness. My fate would have been a life on the margins.

Knowing this, I had long felt a grudge toward my birth country. South Korea did not want children like me, and made sure to get rid of us. Even as I was extremely fortunate in my adoption into a loving family, I resented those who had rejected me. As I got older, I came to understand my birth mother's relinquishment of me as an act of love. And if I squinted very hard, I could even see how my birth father would abandon his own progeny, for in those days it was understood that what soldiers did while stationed abroad was an acceptable consequence of military hegemony, that what happened in Korea stayed in Korea.

But I could not reconcile myself to my country of birth. The South Korean government was complicit in the prostitution that flourished around the camps, not only to keep the US troops happy, but also to introduce much needed foreign currency into a struggling economy. After callously using these women for the country's own gain, the government separated them from their children and then abandoned them, leaving them to a life of shame and neglect, denied the benefits of South Korea's rapid economic advancement that had been built, partially, off their backs.

Returning to Korea on a tour with a group of other mixed-race adoptees, I arrived a day early to search for clues about my origins. I was accompanied by the tour organizer, a Korean woman who is a tireless advocate for Korean adoptees despite having no ties to adoption herself. During our quest, complete strangers went out of their way to help, starting with a woman at a municipal office who spent several hours accompanying us to places where those who might have known my birth mother still resided. People took the time to stop and look at the photo of my birth mother and search their memories back more than fifty years, and to direct us to other people who might have known her. At one point, in a small warren of alleys that housed women who had made their living around the army camps, there was a small parade of elderly women leading us from door to door, just as eager to find my birth mother as I was.

Adoptees must often depend upon the kindness of strangers, starting with the family who adopts them. During the tour, we received these kindnesses daily. The luxury travel bus that took us from one coast of Korea to the other was donated by the owner of the company who personally chauffeured us about for a few days. The city of Bupyeong hosted a lavish banquet for us, complete with entertainment and speeches from dignitaries. The city of Paju has built a park dedicated to adoptees—the first of its kind in the world—a lovely, peaceful spot graced with meaningful art and ringed by a lush fringe of trees. A local restaurant hosted us on two separate occasions, providing ample food and drink as well as cultural experiences. One morning, we feasted on hundreds of dollars' worth of king crab. The list goes on, and there are surely numerous donations of which I was unaware.

In the end, we didn't find my birth mother—this is not that kind of adoption story. But we did find the place where I was born. The building was no longer standing, but there I was, on the very spot where she had once lived, where my birth father had walked from the nearby army base to visit her, where I very likely breathed my first lungful of air, as hospital births were rare at that time. It was a profoundly moving moment, given to me by complete strangers.

As I unpack my suitcase, I notice that some of the gifts are still in their glossy, meticulous wrapping, satin bows still tied tight. I will not hurry to open them because I know it's not about the gift, it's about the gesture. Though I did not find my birth mother, I found something almost as precious, almost as healing: normal, everyday Koreans who showed me love.

Bio

Born in Korea, Alice Stephens was among the first wave of intercountry, transracial adoptees. Her debut novel, *Famous Adopted People*, was published in 2018 by Unnamed Press. Her work has appeared in *LitHub*, the *Los Angeles Review of Books*, *The Margins*, *Banana Writers* and other publications, and has been anthologized in Volume IX of the DC Women's Writers Grace & Gravity series, *Furious Gravity* (2020) and *Writing the Virus* (Outpost19, 2020). She is the editor of *Bloom* and writes book reviews and a column, Alice in Wordland, for the *Washington Independent Review of Books*.

Alice Stephens by James Prochnik

Peiming Sun

Acceptance

Do we really 100% accept ourselves? I have been through a journey that I have finally accepted myself for who I am. Only now, at my 50th year, I start to realize every human being and all other life forms on earth have our unique purpose. Just like one of David Viscott's famous quotes:

"The purpose of life is to discover your gift.

The work of life is to develop it.

The meaning of life is to give your gift away."

Looking back to the 30 years that I lived in the USA as an East-West Navigator, I totally agree with David Viscott's perspective.

In the world of polarities that we live in, life is about a process that is full of crises and opportunities.

I have upgraded myself through this process and accepted what had happened in my past and what will come in the future.

I have used four simple tips for my realization.

Here are the four tips (LOTS as the acronym):

L: Letting go things that were out of my control

My second son was diagnosed with DMD-Duchenne Muscular Dystrophy at age 7. He will be 24 in May 2021; this is definitely a blessing with his condition.

As a single mother and the provider (only source of income), I resigned my work as a scientist in 2008 so that I could stay around to help him more.

Did I feel resentment and sadness for this unexpected challenge I have to go through? YES! Hell YES!!

However, I did not focus on the medical prediction that he would die at a young age; instead I channeled my energy to learn how to help him with his tough journey. I gained so much strength once I let go my worries and negative emotions.

O: Observing things that happening in the present moment

Loved unconditionally by our Source/The Universe, we are provided many opportunities to practice the skill to be in the present.

The present moment is actually the only time that we ever have. The past was gone. The future will be filled with uncertainty. What we think and do NOW can lead to our destiny.

But somehow, we are often unconsciously programmed by the noises/distractions around us by NOT living in the present.

For me, I am lucky to be loaded with LOTS of situations that I could only handle one day at a time.

I have grown this essential skill as a mindful observer so that I can solve problems effectively without getting into an emotional rollercoaster ride.

T: Things are all temporary

Eckhart Tolle mentioned from his book, A New Earth, "All Structures Are Unstable." We create our earth reality via our senses, emotions, and thoughts (just like the movie Matrix).

With Quantum Physics & modern sciences, we now learn things

described in that movie are real human experiences not just ancient opinions from our ancestors.

How lucky that we are in the 21st Century and we are able to grasp an understanding of who we are and what we are capable of!

With this realization, I no longer worry about time and short-term goals.

Instead, I accept my life fully and work toward my higher order with small wins and true joy.

I also feel honored to be a caregiver for an amazing human being who has faced all the challenges and lived to the fullest in his earth life.

As we now know, life is matter and energy.

My son's physical body will vanish soon just like everything goes through the consistent process in the Universe: Birth, Expansion, Contraction, Death then Re-birth.

However, his unique earth existence will stay as a form of eternal energy that has fulfilled its purpose this time around.

S: Serve others

It is our outer purpose (after we accept who we are) to use our unique talents to serve others a.k.a. give our gift away.

As we are all connected in the magnetic field of the Universe, the only way we can all thrive and survive as a global community, is if everyone finds and fulfills their purpose with joy.

Let me use a healthy human body as an analogy. Our body is such an amazing collective of communities that work harmoniously together.

As a biologist, I have always been fascinated about how things work inside the human body. It seems to me that our body has this "Ultimate Sophistication" superpower to operate its business flawlessly.

However, when something in our body goes wrong or loses the internal balance, then we will experience symptoms or discomfort. If we ignore or do not treat these symptoms, they might become part of our chronic conditions that we need to deal with on a daily basis.

Even worse, some cells might be turned into cancerous cells that live to destroy our health rather than contribute to it.

Our earth works the same way. EVERYONE and EVERYTHING in it needs to be healthy and feel safe so that we can build a healthy and thriving global community.

When we are against some who are different or treat them as lower forms of life, it's like an auto-immune disease in our body; we become our own worst enemy. There is no winner when we are against ourselves!

If we are lucky to have unique skills and become sophisticated, it's our calling to give them away and serve as educators through our actions and words for the collective good.

We need to inspire and help others who might be less fortunate to accept who they are and fulfill their roles and functions based on their talents in the global community.

Acceptance.

It's the first step to initiate our amazing transformation. With LOTS, I have healed myself completely in all of life's quadrants: mental, spiritual, physical and financial.

When every single one of us accepts who we are and accepts what others are with compassion, we can reclaim a peaceful, harmonious world that is brightened by the WHITE light: the combination of all colors with their unique frequencies.

I am SUNNY and I accept my role to help with this process and keep shining.

Pei-Ming Sun (aka Sunny)

Ren Yang

The Mask

The Mask was created to accompany a short excerpt written for the 2018 book, *Beneath the Mask: For Teen Adoptees* by the Center for Adoption Support and Education (C.A.S.E.). The book is a compilation of writings by adoptees for adoptees. The Mask represents the feeling of being somewhere between two drastically different cultures: too Chinese in the U.S. but too American when in China. Is there a way for these complementary sides to coexist? The hands reaching out to each other from opposite circles portray the challenges and effort it has taken to learn how to juggle these two cultural identities. Around the border of The Mask reads a quote by Karen Brown Belanger which goes, "If I told you I lost my mother at birth, the usual reaction is one of sympathy. If I told you I was adopted, the usual reaction is how wonderful. It's the same thing." The only facial features included are the eyes, emphasizing that a lot of the challenges and struggles that can come with being adopted are much deeper than what the surface dares reveal.

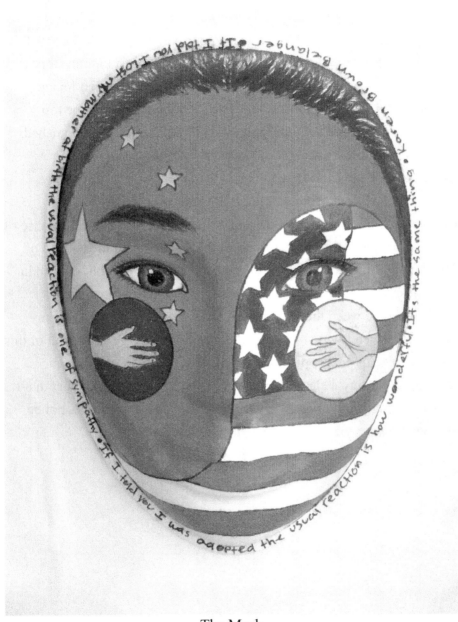

The Mask

The Scroll

Completed in 2014 and measuring approximately 16x50 inches, this mixed media scroll portrays what I understand of my adoption story in China and utilizes acrylics, puzzle pieces, charcoal, personal image rubbings and an old window blind. The family portrayed at the top represents my theoretical birthparents and I before being relinquished. Made to resemble a propaganda poster, the Chinese characters immediately below are there to mass persuade the one-child policy. Presumably, with the combination of the one-child policy and the traditional Chinese cultural favoring of boys, I am abandoned because of my gender. It is at this time the puzzle breaks apart and the collage of faded images in-between illustrates what little I know about my life in the orphanage until I eventually was adopted. The four images sandwiched between the two puzzles are actually photos taken at my orphanage when I was still there. But questions emerge as a result of this swirling haze of puzzle pieces around my head attempting to come together to portray a clear picture. Unable to settle due to the fact that I know nothing about my past except that I was left in front of a police station, my past will forever be an incomplete puzzle.

The Scroll

Bio

Ren Yang was born in 1996 and spent her first three years in an orphanage in Yangzhou, China. In 1999, Ren was adopted into a transracial family and has lived most of her life in Maryland. From the first time she was given a crayon back in the hotel room in China where she met her forever mother, Ren has been forever enthralled by drawing and creating art. Throughout schooling and beyond, Ren has always turned to art when grappling with sensitive topics such as adoption and identity. Ren, more often than not, finds communicating her thoughts, feelings and experiences through visual art more effective than through words. Currently a second semester junior at the University of Maryland, Ren is focusing her studies on Studio Art and Mandarin.

Christine Phan

Loving Me for Who I Am

We're nearing the end of May which is Asian Pacific American Heritage Month (APAHM). For the longest time, I've wanted to tell my story as an Asian American, and while it's not particularly unique, I'm sure there is someone out there who will be able to relate a little bit.

To give you context, my parents are Vietnamese immigrants who came to the United States in 1992. Neither of them spoke English, but fast forward 28 years later and they both have jobs where they speak English all the time. In 1993, my sister was born, and shortly after, they moved to Albuquerque, New Mexico. I was born in Albuquerque in 1998, and have spent the last 21 years of my life here.

I remember the first time I realized I was *different* was in the second grade. My earliest memory of this was when one of my classmates asked me if I was Japanese? Chinese? I told him no, I'm Vietnamese. I remember kids running up to me on the playground, pulling their eyes back and saying "Ching-chong, ching-chong," but not feeling too bothered by it. In fact, I did it, too.

In middle school, I distinctly remember asking my mom to make me "American food," or food that I wouldn't be embarrassed to eat in front of my friends. Some days, I would even choose to skip lunch altogether to avoid the possibility of being judged. I remember hearing jokes about eating dogs and even making those jokes myself. I remember when classmates would attribute my successes to the sole fact that I was Asian. I didn't realize just how much these things hurt me. It wouldn't be until years later that I realized that this was what they call "internalized racism." I didn't begin to unlearn this internalized racism until years later in eighth grade.

Going to a predominantly White school and being one of the only Asian students in the entire school was hard. I felt like I didn't fit in, and even though I had friends, I couldn't always relate to them. While they talked about how they got iPods and J.Crew sweaters for Christmas, I sat there quietly, envying their parents' money and wondering why my parents didn't love me the way theirs did. What a horrible, awful thought I could have had, right? Well, it explains why at times, I wanted to run away and be adopted by a rich, White family. Or even the times I wanted to *be* White. It was hard to accept, much less embrace, my identity as a young pre-teen who was just looking to fit in. I often thought boys liked my friends more than they liked me because not only was I ugly, but I was ugly because I was Asian. The internalized racism built up and ate away at me during some of the most formative years of my life. I was self-conscious, insecure, and lonely.

I always wanted Asian friends who could relate to me, Asian friends who ate with chopsticks, who could pronounce my name, who liked K-pop like me and didn't think it was weird or foreign. What I craved was a person who could understand me and what I was going through; still, I want to make it clear that I do not fault my friends for any of this. If I can't change who I am, how can they? It was simply chance that put me where I was, but with all things, I believe everything happens for a reason. In fact, I think being around so many non-Asians strengthened my connection to my roots and identity (after I started unlearning all of that racism, of course).

While being Vietnamese is very much a core part of my identity, it does not solely define who I am. While I do like various Asian foods, snacks, watch K-dramas and K-pop, anime, etc., these things do not make me any *more* Asian, nor does loving brunch, watching American TV shows, or getting B's in school make me any *less* Asian. These are just my traits and hobbies, and that's just who I am as a person. There is so much more to me than meets the eye, and even I have yet to fully discover myself and the things I truly am passionate about. But one thing is clear: I am who I am. Sam, I am. Just kidding, I'm Christine.

My journey of self-love and acceptance has been everything but smooth. But it's a journey I'm glad to be taking because I'm not quite sure who I would be today if not for fully embracing the fact that I'm awesome just the way I am. It's not easy, but hey, when has a life worth living been easy?

Gradually, I became more interested in Asian American history and politics, and more politically informed in general. My identity is inherently political, and I want to make that clear. I am standing on the shoulders of people who have **fought** for my **right** to be here, to exist and call this country home. In these unprecedented times, we have seen an increase in hate crimes against Asians in America. It is important to stand in solidarity, not just with our fellow Asians and Asian Americans, but also the Black and Latinx communities who are fighting for *all of us*. We must all put in the work to demand better from a system that was designed to not only hold us back, but also pit us against one another. This is about demanding better for all of us, because no matter how good something might be, it's never enough. The opposite is true, too: If something is enough that doesn't always mean that it's good.

We are not free until we are all free.

For as long as other communities are struggling and experiencing injustice, we must stand and fight for them, too, just as they have stood and fought for us.

Being Asian American goes beyond representation in Hollywood and smelly lunches. It means finding the strength, the courage, and the bravery to stand side-by-side with one another. It means recognizing, naming, and fighting injustice as it happens. Being Asian American means **love**; loving yourself so that you can love others because it is harder to love than hate. We fear what we do not know, so now is our chance to take this time to *learn*. Being Asian American means taking every experience that we have and using it as a learning opportunity for ourselves, for others, and for the generations to come. The work we put in, no matter how big or small, will surely impact our future whether we know it now or not.

I hope that this month, you can reflect on what being Asian American means to you, and that you continue to love and embrace your background with an open mind, and an open heart.

Rufina C. Garay

Nothing Wasted

When I think of Chinese cookery,
I picture the economy of a scallion, the high yield
of the purest white and pale green parts, stir fried.
Bias-cut, dark green tops, all thin to garnish soy and vinegar sauce.
Add garlic. Almost always, add garlic.
Left behind are the small grassy roots just as slender,
Compost for the earth.
Returning is the motion of the Tao.
To me, Chinese cookery means nothing wasted,
Everything and everyone valued,
'Round the kitchen watching matriarchs and masters cook,
'Round the table, eating, laughing.
Chicken dinner's not yet truly done,
Until the cartilage is gnawed,
Still to come,
Roast the bones until dark,
when the marrow runs dry
*Like the blood of my elder, 84-year-old Mr. Vicha, tackled to his death on
    a "regular morning walk" in "misty Northern California."*
"Make soup with the bones," says my mother's voice inside my head.
Nothing wasted.
*In the oven, the carcass sits while I am empty like the hollow of its chest
    cavity. Our ribs heave silent sighs, browned.*
How do we make soup with these dead bones?
Even chicken feet are more valued, not thrown away
But frozen together
With others,
then unthawed

transformed to stock
or even better,
authentic
healing
bone broth.
Nothing wasted.
But here, today not one Chinaman is valued.
A ripped shirt reveals
This military patriot's scars,
important to him.
Alone.
All the same now.
Fathers and grandfathers
Already built your railroads,
Ushered in the American Manifest Destiny
at a discount.
All discarded.
Denied their blistered American citizenry daily
because of the slant of their eyes.
In wartime, camps opened, holding a mirror to overseas horror,
one step shy of the enemy, justifying
citizens held captive by their own government.
Why not weep for a sin-less Sisyphus
who eternally slides back down the hill of
betrayal and loss?
You're taking too many bones.
You're making too many bones.
"I can't breathe," became "We can't breathe" a long time ago.
No words wasted
for a man, woman, or child from Japan
until the too-late apology.
Korematsu's justice came forty-four years—a lifetime—too late
His personal diaspora drove him Eastward.

But, thank Tao that Korematsu spoke his words.
You can scarcely appreciate the economy of a scallion, until your bones
*   are cracked*
Or hollowed out from what you see and feel.
Returning is the motion of the Tao.
Tie the horses to the post.
Nothing wasted.
But maybe our breath.
— ©2021 Rufina C. Garay. All rights reserved.

Acting as Though

Acting as though I'm not disappointed in people or disgusted with a few
  makes me tired.
Acting as though disconnection could be made whole by Zooms and
  infrequent phone calls that have less and less meaning and more and
  more performance, makes the struggle of extroverting my daily
  stumbling block,
Because I need what little there is to get from the halo of it all.
Acting as though I don't have rage over the egos of
gatekeepers held up with ivory hands to win prizes for excellence
makes me exhausted,
even terrified
the way certain seers imagined—
knew what atomic bombs going off
would do when they struck inhabited land,
rupturing, then melting skin that wasn't theirs—didn't look like them,
to protect something very important.
Acting as though it doesn't bother me that people pat themselves on the
  back
for attending this training,
doing this good and recognized deed,
reading this or that book,
when they forget that relationships with real people actually matter,
makes me realize that I have grown older.
I would hold each person, including myself more accountable, with or
  without hashtags.
I ask
how I can contribute in,
how can I collaborate from an authentic place?
I won't give up until the real women of excellence show up or are given
  access to the stage.
I have to hold on to the identity I know, resting below the surface of the
  blood boiling.

Wind invading wood phase produces imbalance, anger in the liver,
but not just anger.

Rage. Rage over a number of years.

Rage over a White woman talking to me through her misperceptions of
    my point of view while I wait patiently.

She is ready for everyone else to be wrong.

Rage over the righteousness she wears like a blazoned red cape. I gently
    explain that she has assumed something incorrectly.

She assumes everyone is always talking about oppression.

My first generation cousin who is of no blood relationship to me would
    tell this activist that she has made an "Ass-(out of)-u-(and) me."

As if, my focus on hierarchies of access to foster empowerment was her
    idea.

She is blind to the entanglement of her ego in the work.

She isn't ready to pass the mic to our dark sister, or to pay her to lead.

She is comfortable as the voice, the leading "do-gooder." But her
    challenge is simply to *be better*.

She is the younger version of the gatekeeper. These women of
    excellence know a lot. If you are from my parents' country of origin,
    you will know what I mean by this.

As if, she had my lived experience.

Only the wind of tsunamis can imagine the destruction I could produce
    with my tongue.

I hold it.

I promise to breathe in his honor instead.

I see no stranger*, but the more you laud yourselves, the less I can feel
    the spirit of this great work, and the more I see the return of self-
    absorption.

That momentary pause for reflection in that original pivot slips away.
    The terror of

"I can't breathe"

is yesterday's news to you.

Couldn't you hold on to it for one moment more before saying goodbye?

Kiss that lover who melted every ice wall you put up

who soaked in your vulnerabilities as if they were shared, lived-in skin
whose bruises and sores were not too much to handle, and who
tended to those wounds with every gentle caress?

No. You are back to surviving in the literal wake of others not like you.

My elders dying on the streets from hate crimes are simply foreign to
you, distanced by how you take refuge in focusing first on one thing.
You abdicate your responsibilities to see and share from your seat of
authority, from your place of privilege.

Yesterday, those hate crimes were your post-election, ineffective
hashtags.

Then, you let him, the White terrorist whose face you've already seen
multiple times, slaughter my sisters. He is your progeny.

It matters that I, as an Asian (as you call me), or rather, as a Chinese-
Filipino-Spanish American (as I know me), want to focus first on the
fundamental truth that

Black Lives Matter.

It matters that we model for others what it means to show up

and take a stand for each other,

how we do that with the different colors and

shades of skin we inhabit.

It matters too that my dark and sacred sister will know how to speak of
my precious elders, even if you cannot.

In grace, her blood boils too, and she will give space to it.

She knows the sorrow of my silent sisters, their sons, daughters, and
children.

But you women of excellence, must you show up brightest at the table
with the greenest adornments, gleaming gold now in the shroud of
my sisters?

Must you be the arbiter of whose mind matters, whose hearts we care
about, and whose spirits we crush? Why do you show up with so
little appreciation for others?

Must all the people of color line up in a neat and orderly queue so that you can handle it,

so you can process how to focus?

The earth in all her complexity does not tell the grass to stop growing in
order for the apple, pear, plum, and quince trees to bear fruit.

There is a time and season for it all.

There is a time and season for us all to bear fruit.

Follow mother nature to know endless bounty,

remembrance and respect for every living being

and a resting place for that which is dead.

Having no place to put this dis-ease of discontent with humanity where
once I had such unbridled and deep love, I can only offer it to the
magnificence of water.

Pull it away from me in low tide,

wash me in imagined forgiveness

until rage runs shallow

leaving only jutting rocks and pebbles

until the emptiness becomes as real as the sun's violet rays

reflecting its intensity at dusk at that perfect angle

where the blurred brightness below opens like a peaceful portal to the
hidden beauty and danger of what could swallow us up.

— © 2021 Rufina C. Garay, J.D. All Rights Reserved.

*"see no stranger" is a concept from the Sikh Muslim tradition shared by
activist and civil rights lawyer, Valarie Kaur, who advocates for
revolutionary love.

Bio

Rufina C. Garay is an executive leadership coach, business strategist, attorney, qi gong instructor, mediator, chef, and artist who promotes diversity, equity, inclusion, and belonging through her multi-faceted work. Her coaching practice is dedicated to empowering women and people of color who are emergent or established leaders. She specializes in facilitating group discussions on matters of race that meets people where they are currently in their thinking and in spirit. She teaches fundamental conflict resolution skills and offers communication interventions to help people of any color have meaningful conversations on inclusion. The aftermath of George Floyd's murder compounded by anti-Asian race-related murders and assaults led to her desire to give voice to undercurrents of rage masked by silence at the surface. She believes that creativity is the path to an imagined, fully inclusive future. Spoken word and visual art are meditative practices for her that can facilitate important conversations and transformation.

Rufina graduated as a Tony Patiño Fellow from Columbia University School of Law and *cum laude* from Amherst College with a double major in Russian language and literature and English literature. She is an alumna of Duke University's Biotechnology for Business Program and Dartmouth's Tuck Diversity Program. In addition, Rufina is an alumna of New England Culinary Institute.

Rufina's commitment to equity has led her to serve on the Board of Directors of many organizations, including Jefferson County Farmers Market Board of Directors and Greater Good (an affiliate of the national fiscal sponsorship organization Social Good Fund). She also serves as a member of the Food System Resiliency Task Force which focuses on food security. She recently launched a podcast called FoodLove: The Space Between Terroir and the Tao of Food that spotlights food as an access point to talk about matters of culture, race, equity, social and environmental justice, art, self-expression, community, and peace.

As a certified qigong instructor and practitioner of Tai Chi, Rufina has a holistic approach to coaching. Her approach is facilitative and balanced, informed by what has brought each client or group to the particular moment of leadership, change, challenge, or opportunity.

Tong (Toni) Liu, MD

"Thank you so much, I've been trying to tell them but they didn't understand," my Chinese patient sighed with relief. I was one of the few physicians of color at that clinic, and the only one who spoke Mandarin. I looked back on her previous visit notes, alarmed by the inaccuracies in the history-taking sections. Her English was fair, but she was able to express herself so much more fully when able to use her native tongue. I felt a wave of gratitude that I could help her finally get to the root of this issue and a sense of pride for being able to serve as this bridge over the language gap.

As an Asian-American who immigrated at age 3, I am quite Americanized. I grew up in a traditional, strict Chinese family on the east coast, attended a very liberal college and medical school, and since then have been drawn to getting to know all other cultures as a globe-hopping digital nomad.

Many are surprised when I can speak Mandarin fluently since many young immigrants do not keep up their native language or cultural roots. I made a conscious effort because my Chinese background is so important to me. It's a piece of my family and our unique ancestry. It enriches me with its values of cooperation, harmony, and sacrifice. It helps me think more compassionately as a global citizen - when there are 2 worlds within me, it's impossible for me to take the stand of any one side.

I had always been proud to call myself Chinese, even opting to answer the question "Where are you from?" with "China" when abroad, especially during Trump's presidency, when I felt embarrassed to be an American. I had voted and done my due diligence, but I was so ashamed that we allowed someone like Trump to take power.

Then the Covid-19 pandemic added stigma, challenge, and difficulty to the other half of me. Never had I been more afraid of being myself, taking up space, or making my voice heard, as now both halves of me were stigmatized and unwelcome by more people than ever. I had already experienced plenty of bullying and abuse for being fat, "ungirly"/tomboy-ish, nerdy, awkward, quiet, shy...those experiences kept myself small for most of my life.

News of hate crimes, bullying, and discrimination flooded me every day with more victims, of both overt and subtle prejudice. More Asians and other persons of color were dying from the pandemic at alarmingly disproportionate rates, 26-53% (Asians the highest). Some of it may be due to cultural customs such as saving face, not complaining and pushing on on one's own so as not to burden others, leading many to seek help too late.

But some were likely also due to discrimination from providers. As a healthcare worker myself, previously in obstetrics and now primary care, I had witnessed firsthand the disparities of care towards persons of color, especially African Americans, on the labor floor, leading to higher morbidity and mortality for mothers. They were assumed to be "always angry" and their medical complaints not taken as seriously, leading to later diagnoses of life-threatening illnesses. The language barriers for patients whose native tongues are not English also play a role, as my time at that clinic revealed.

We've tried to assimilate but it will never be completely. Our accents, our values, our beliefs, some parts of our history and the generations before us will always remain. Intergenerational trauma was passed down to us through our epigenetics; it is real, potent, and painful.

We have faced so much from being the Other in this new land, never fully accepted. Ignored for a while as we try to quietly do good work from the shadows, and now brought back into the light in the most negative way possible. A racist president labeling a disease "The Chinese Virus" set back decades of progress towards equality, inclusion, acceptance, and peace. Yes, we have not had it as rough as other minority groups, but that doesn't mean our story and our experiences are any less valid.

It brought so much sadness and despair when I realized America was not quite the melting pot or land of opportunity I had always been told it would be. My parents constantly remind me of how they came here to give me a better life and list out all their sacrifices. They sometimes use it to try to guilt me into staying in medicine. I had finally taken a stand for myself as an individual 3 years ago when I left traditional medicine to pursue my true passions of art and healing through a way that felt more aligned and authentic to me (life coaching).

I have my American side to thank for that, as I probably would not have dared to do such a thing had we stayed in China. I am truly grateful for the experiences I've had, the opportunities I've been given, and recognize and appreciate what my family has done for me. But I don't have to keep sacrificing myself and my soul just to keep the peace, make my ancestors proud, or take on the entire responsibility of another person's happiness.

In fact, it would honor my ancestors MORE if I allowed myself to blossom into the fullest version of myself, by being true to my heart and following these inexplicable urges to serve the world in my own creative way. To honor my childhood dreams before all the fear and anxiety bled into them, to serve from a place of pure love, rather than fear.

Recent events have brought to the forefront the worst of human behavior and shed light on all that we still need to work on. At a surface level we have many immigrants and multicultural citizens in this country, but we haven't yet learned how to create a fully safe, supportive environment to celebrate differentness rather than sameness.

We're far from perfect, but this is all we have, right? What better place to start change to push for more diversity and inclusion than here, the most diverse of countries? I had been torn about relocating to somewhere I would be more accepted vs. staying to fight for the world I dream of. But with the Internet, I can advocate for change no matter where I am. Because it doesn't matter where I physically am; I am everywhere because my home is in my heart and that is infinite and can reach to every part of our Universe.

I am Asian but I am also an American. I am a human. I am a citizen of the Earth. We all came from one country, before the lands split and water got in between them, but we are still all one planet, and we are all connected. I suffer when my brothers and sisters suffer. Why do we keep hurting others out of fear or ignorance? Why do we point fingers or always try to find someone to blame? We all have some responsibility in what's happening in our world and we each have so much power to change it. We will run into challenges and obstacles, but we are so much more effective as one team.

I am not the enemy. No living soul is. I love and care about you even if I've never met you. You being alive, with your own unique passions, hopes, dreams, talents, makes you WORTHY of love and respect. I'm fighting for the day when we all realize we have so much more in common than we do differences. We all want love, belonging, purpose, meaning, joy, to seek pleasure and avoid pain.

What would it be like if we all embraced our humanity and saw each other as the beautiful gifts that we are, housed in different wrapping papers? Our souls are what matter, not our shells. We are more alike than we think and all it takes is the curiosity and openness to ask, to learn, to try to get to know. And listen.

Tong (Toni) Liu, MD

Bio

Tong (Toni) Liu is a Chinese-American board-certified family physician, former gynecologist, cartoonist, life + relationship coach, blogger, and global nomad. She empowers, educates, and advocates for women, persons of color, and other minorities, with missions of authenticity, wellness, sexual liberation, inclusion, universal love and acceptance. She's extremely passionate about social justice, women's reproductive rights, sex education, holistic health, challenging toxic cultural traditions, and living true to one's heart. Her hobbies include traveling, racquet sports, ultimate frisbee, skiing, dance, cooking/baking, learning languages, sketching, and anything outdoors.

Kathie Shiba

After the Atlanta Shootings

Facebook, March 22nd, 2021

Thank you for accepting me into this group. Here are highlights of
my life story. I am of Japanese heritage, a sansei, born to parents who, as
a teenager and a young adult, were imprisoned in concentration camps
during WWII. As a direct result of that (yes it impacted us across
generations), I was raised to not stand out, to not make noise, to keep my
head down and work hard, to endure. And I have endured much
throughout my 65 years of life - taunts, laughter, name calling,
inappropriate touching, and so much more. These were directed to me
because of the reactions of others to my Asian heritage - being
sexualized, being eroticized, being made invisible, being silenced, being
asked to represent the Asian perspective, and so much more. I've been
criticized for my reactions - "you're overreacting," "you're too passive,"
"it's not racism," "get control of your emotions," "do something," "stay
in your lane," and so much more. and so much more. I am proud of my
life story, of my achievements, of earning my Ph.D., of being the first
woman of Asian heritage who is chair of a division at my college, of
surviving Acute Myeloid Leukemia and a stem cell transplant, of raising
two strong and loving children, of mentoring college students and
showing them what a strong, intelligent woman of Asian heritage is like.
As I reflect on my 65 years of life, I am indeed proud of being the
daughter of parents who endured and survived much throughout their
lives, as they lived the reality of being prisoners behind barbed wires, of
being placed in poorly constructed "buildings" with no privacy, of
seeing the shame and anguish of their own parents, of feeling the shame

themselves and transmitting that shame to their own children, and yet who demonstrated their bravery, tenacity, and persistence as they made a life for my three siblings and me. Yes, I am proud - of my Asian heritage, of being Japanese American, and so much more.

Bio

Kathie Shiba, Ph. D., is a professor of psychology and chair of the Division of Behavioral Sciences at Maryville College. She is a self-proclaimed foodie, a Unitarian Universalist, a student of Buddhism and yoga, a peace lover, and a life-long learner. She lives in Maryville, Tennessee with her husband, son, dog, and two cats, while her daughter and partner live in Lafayette, Louisiana ... and they all affectionately call her peacekat.

Kathie Shiba, Ph.D.

Kathie Shiba with Sophie

Suzanne Gilbert

I am an ally ©

I am an ally.

That means, for me, that I get you in two ways but I also get that I am not living in your shoes.

I get you on principled grounds: we are both Americans, both worthy of love, respect, and inclusion. That's a keystone fact, keystone being the key from which other facts flow.

But I also reach to get it on a more personal level. That's a keystone fact as well. I grew up outside my ancestral heritage. Most of my ancestors and I, if we were to meet through time travel, wouldn't be able to talk to each other; we don't share a language. What's more, my heritage wasn't taught in public school history books as part of America. Learning more about my heritage was a decision I made in adulthood, although my parents did their best.

Another keystone fact is that the kids I would die for are bi-racial, their father being ethnic Hakka Chinese from Thailand. That made us a conspicuous family, not only because some of us were Asian, but because we were transracial and mixed race. There were years of my life when I read, wrote, spoke, and dreamed in an East Asian language yet felt the sting of discrimination in that country I loved. The main thing I learned, though, to help me be an ally, is that despite the discrimination I faced as a foreigner there, I could always come home to white privilege in America.

Another keystone fact is that I love this country despite its laws and regulations that discriminated against people like me. They allowed social workers to lie to my adoptive parents in order to hide my true heritage, and to not privilege people of my same race when they placed me in a foster or adoptive home. My heritage is Cherokee and Mohawk and, until the Indian Child Welfare Act of 1978, what happened to me was common practice.

I'm also part Jewish in an age when even our first BIPOC president, Barack Obama, wrote in his memoir that America is a Christian country [pp. 121,]. It makes me want to add one more letter to the alphabet army and call us BIJPOC (Black Indigenous Jewish People of Color). I don't care if East Asians, South Asians, and Jews are considered affluent; we're smart, sexy, and successful – yes – but also compensating for being the Other.

Another keystone fact is that if you emigrated here through adoption, I get that too. I also know what it's like to travel overseas to meet my mother for the first time in my thirties, and to have to book a plane every time after then when I want to see, hear, and hold my first blood relation. Humans aren't hatched, we were carried for nine months, and the loss of that mammalian connection through our formative years is real and matters.

I also get how the savior complex plays out, you know, where

the white parents are assumed

to have saved the BIPOC child

who is therefore supposed to feel lucky to be relinquished.

Sometimes the savior complex plays out very publicly for our conspicuous families:

My mother, sister, and I were shopping in Target one day. My son was sitting in the cart, and my four-year old daughter was standing nearby when an older white woman came up to her. The stranger leaned down and asked a question.

"Are you and your brother adopted?"

My child didn't miss a beat, "No, my brother, grandma, and I aren't. But my mom and aunt are."

The poor old lady was very confused. No one ever asked her – or my sister and me – whether we were adopted because we present as white.

~ *Suzanne Gilbert*

https://www.amazon.com/author/suzannegilbert

Bio

One afternoon in 1991 when her adoptive mom dropped by, Suzanne Gilbert got an international phone call from London that no one expected. England had unsealed its adoption records fifteen years earlier and it was her birthmother calling. Thus began a journey for both her moms and Suzanne and the search for her birthfather.

To this Suzanne brings experience as a story producer for ABC News in Boston and Tokyo, as well as an ongoing career in tech & cybersecurity journalism under her adoptive name. In addition, she is a 20-year cybersecurity veteran (which means she cracks mysteries).

Suzanne would eventually fall in love with an adoptive father of three boys and she would help raise them as their "third mom". The triple role of adoptive step mom, adoptee in reunion, and avid reader eventually led to her curating virtual bookshelves of several hundred works of adoption fiction and non-fiction, including movies, music, novels, and poetry.

--She is focusing on her adoption-acquired skills in investigative genetic genealogy (IGG), her computer forensics background, and love of writing to create a series of cyber crime mysteries. In the non-fiction realm she is editing a book on the 12 Steps as well as one on reunions.

Suzanne Gilbert

* * *

Made in the USA
Middletown, DE
05 June 2021

40634664R00159